The American League

The American League

An Illustrated History

by Donald Honig

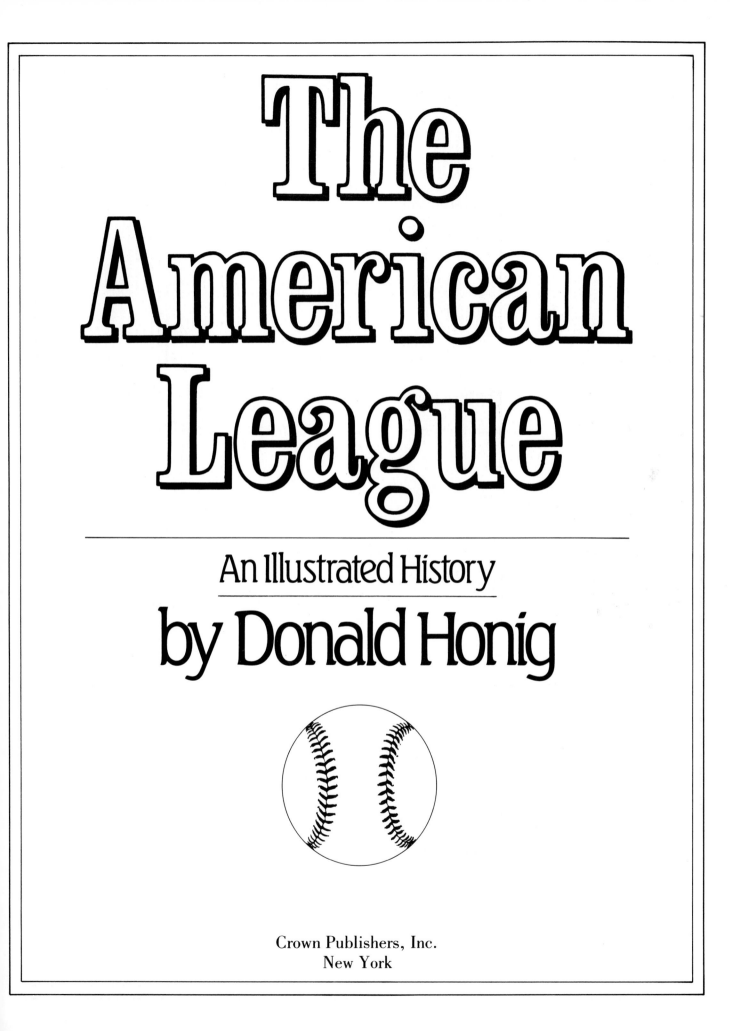

Crown Publishers, Inc.
New York

Published by Crown Publishers, Inc., One Park Avenue, New York, New York 10016,
and simultaneously in Canada by General Publishing Company Limited

Manufactured in the United States of America

Library of Congress Cataloging in Publication Data

Honig, Donald.
The American League.

Includes index.
1. American League of Professional Baseball Clubs—
History. I. Title.
GV875.A15H66 1983   796.357′64′0973   83-2006
ISBN 0-517-55042-3

10 9 8 7 6 5 4 3 2 1

First Edition

Design: Robert Aulicino

For my daughter, Catherine

By Donald Honig

Fiction

Sidewalk Caesar
Walk Like a Man
The Americans
Divide the Night
No Song to Sing
Judgment Night
The Love Thief
The Severith Style
Illusions
I Should Have Sold Petunias
The Last Great Season
Marching Home

Nonfiction

Baseball When the Grass Was Real
Baseball Between the Lines
The Man in the Dugout
The October Heroes
The Image of Their Greatness (with Lawrence Ritter)
The 100 Greatest Baseball Players of All Time (with Lawrence Ritter)
The Brooklyn Dodgers: An Illustrated Tribute
The New York Yankees: An Illustrated History
Baseball's 10 Greatest Teams
The Los Angeles Dodgers: The First Quarter Century
The National League: An Illustrated History
The American League: An Illustrated History

For Young Readers

Frontiers of Fortune
Jed McLane and Storm Cloud
Jed McLane and the Stranger
In the Days of the Cowboy
Up from the Minor Leagues
Dynamite
Johnny Lee
The Journal of One Davey Wyatt
An End of Innocence
Way to Go Teddy
Playing for Keeps
Breaking In
The Professional
Coming Back
Fury on Skates
Hurry Home
Running Harder
Going the Distance
Winter Always Comes

Editor

Blue and Gray: Great Writings of the Civil War
The Short Stories of Stephen Crane

Contents

Acknowledgments

I am deeply indebted to a number of people for their generous assistance in photo research and help in gathering the photographs reproduced in this book. Special thanks are due Jack Redding, librarian of the National Baseball Hall of Fame, for his interest, his expertise, and his help. Also, to Michael P. Aronstein, president of the Card Memorabilia Associates, Ltd., in Amawalk, New York, for the generosity of his assistance and the unique wisdom and spirited enthusiasm he brings to his work. I would also like to thank those big-league ballplayers who allowed the use of pictures from their personal albums.

Also, for their guidance and advice, the author is indebted to the following: Andrew Aronstein, David Markson, Lawrence Ritter, Stanley Honig, Jean Kozlowski, Mary E. Gallagher, and Allan J. Grotheer.

The following photos are from the following sources:
J. J. Donnelly, Pearl River, New York: pp. 294, 299, 302 (right), 304, 305 (bottom right), 306 (right), 308, 309 (right), 310 (top left and right), 311 (left and top right), 314, 316 (top right), 318 (top right), 320 (right), 321 (left, top right, bottom right), 322 (bottom left), 324 (top left), 325 (top left, bottom left), 326 (bottom), 330 (left, bottom right), 331.
Nancy Hogue, Warren, Ohio: pp. 310 (bottom), 313 (top right), 317, 318 (left), 320 (bottom left), 322 (top left), 325 (right), 326 (top), 327, 328, 330 (top right), 332 (left, bottom right), 333.
Ronald C. Modra, Port Washington, Wisconsin: pp. 295 (bottom), 301, 302 (left), 303 (bottom), 306 (left), 307 (bottom), 309 (left), 311 (bottom right), 313 (left), 315, 316 (left), 319, 322 (right), 323, 324 (bottom left), 329, 332 (top right).

The American League

Ban Johnson.

1

Beginning

Beginning in 1876 and for a quarter century thereafter, the National League was the dominant force in professional baseball, its strength constantly increasing as the game began taking root in the national imagination. By 1900, the eight-club structure that remained intact until 1952 was in effect.

From time to time the National League's preeminence came under challenge. In 1882 an outfit called the American Association was organized, declared itself a major league, and stayed in business until 1891. In 1884 the Union Association tried to muscle in and lasted but one season. Similarly, the Players' League came and went in a single season, 1890. The National League outlasted them all, and as the century turned, the league's supremacy over America's favorite game seemed complete and unchallengeable.

The dream of starting a new major league, however, had for at least a decade been agitating the imagination of one Byron Bancroft Johnson, known to one and all as "Ban." Tough, vain, heavy-handed, by all accounts anything but a cuddly personality (typical, it seems, of America's entrepreneurial go-getters of the time), Johnson was convinced he could succeed where others had failed.

In 1893 the twenty-nine-year-old Johnson, a native of Norwalk, Ohio, was president of the Western League, the strongest of the minor leagues, with clubs scattered through the Midwest. Running the St. Paul franchise in Johnson's circuit was Charles Comiskey, formerly a first baseman in the recently defunct American Association. Together, Johnson and Comiskey uncorked many a bottle while sitting and discussing baseball's future. These two visionaries of the game's pioneer years agreed to keep upgrading their league until they were ready to declare it a major league.

In those years baseball had a reputation for rowdyism, both in the stands and on the field. Johnson moved to take firm control of his league and his product. The sale of liquor in ball parks was banned, profanity was discouraged, the authority of umpires was strictly upheld. Women, infrequent spectators at baseball games in those days, were encouraged to come out and enjoy a diverting nine innings. Western League games became an increasingly more pleasant afternoon's recreation, and soon almost every franchise in the league was thriving.

Convinced he was ready to make his move to compete as a major league, Johnson in 1900 made an implicit broadening of geographical scope by renaming his circuit the American League. A year later he declared it a major league.

Not only did Johnson shed his league's regional character, but he did so with daring and emphasis—placing franchises in three National League cities: Chicago, Boston, and Philadelphia. The other five outposts in the original American League were located in Detroit, Baltimore, Washington, Cleveland, and Milwaukee. A year later St. Louis replaced Milwaukee, and a year after that, in 1903, New York replaced Baltimore. This alignment remained undisturbed until 1954. With St. Louis and New York also being National League cities, by 1903 the two leagues were in nose-to-nose competition in five of their eight cities.

Naturally, the National League was less than delighted with the new competition. Not only were they indignant and outraged, but they were also apprehensive. Ban Johnson was not an unknown quantity. Vain, arrogant, and autocratic he may have been; impetuous he was not. He was a man who toed the turf judiciously before putting his full weight forward. The National League club owners knew that the competition was well heeled, prepared to spend heavily, well organized, and determined. The Nationals also knew

that in order to give their league credibility, the Americans were going to need star players. And everyone knew where these players were casting their shadows—in the National League.

Johnson and his colleagues decided to ignore the reserve clause in the National League's player contracts—the reserve clause being the ball and chain in every contract binding the player to the club until the club decided to sever the link.

In order to entice the players out of their contractual obligations, the new league had to unfold some heavy cash. The classic temptation started a migration from one league to the other. Among some of the classy names whose pockets got the itch were pitchers Cy Young and Joe McGinnity and infielders Napoleon Lajoie, Jimmy Collins, and John McGraw. The $2,400-yearly-salary ceiling that the National League, secure in its monopoly, had established made it easier for these knights of the diamond and many lesser players to reach for their suitcases.

With National League rosters defenseless against the locust attacks of the newcomers, and with the American League operating full blast in 1901, the dispute moved to the courts. The National League won the first skirmish when the Pennsylvania Supreme Court upheld the legality of the reserve clause and ordered Lajoie back to the Philadelphia National League club, from whence he had jumped. But since this order carried weight only in the state of Pennsylvania, the crafty Johnson transferred Nap's contract from the Philadelphia Athletics to the Cleveland club. This meant that when Cleveland came to Philadelphia to play, Lajoie couldn't participate; but it also meant that the game's top hitter remained in the American League.

The courts in other states involved in the dispute, however, declared against the reserve clause, establishing the legitimacy of the new contracts.

Moving with impunity now, the American

League continued picking the juiciest apples from National League trees. Star players like shortstop Bobby Wallace and outfielders Jesse Burkett and Ed Delahanty succumbed to the new dollar-green pastures. They were soon joined by luminaries such as pitchers Jack Chesbro and Wild Bill Donovan, and outfielders Sam Crawford and Wee Willie Keeler.

After two seasons of open warfare, the National League came to accept the inevitable: the American League was here to stay. This was not just an opinion either—the newcomers were showing healthy attendance figures, outdrawing the Nationals in Boston, Chicago, and Philadelphia by significant margins.

Following the close of the 1902 season, the two leagues opened peace talks. Initially, the National League sought a merger between the two circuits, but Ban Johnson was opposed; he finally had himself a thriving, fully accepted, and recognized major league, and he preferred keeping it that way. His club owners backed him to the hilt. One of those owners, in Chicago, was Charles Comiskey. Managing Comiskey's White Sox was Clark Griffith; and managing the Philadelphia Athletics was Connie Mack. These three men, whose names go resounding through American League history like Founding Fathers, were destined to influence the league for the next half century.

The peace talks amounted to a substantial American League victory. Johnson got everything he wanted: recognition as a major league, respect for the reserve clause in the contracts of the players his league had signed, and permission to keep practically all the players pirated from the National League. Johnson also won the right to place a team in New York, something bitterly opposed by John McGraw, now managing the Giants. The only concession the American League made was to promise not to put a team in Pittsburgh.

A national commission was formed. The function of this three-man board was to rule on disputes between clubs and between clubs and players. The members were Johnson; the president of the National League; and Garry Herrmann, owner of the Cincinnati Reds. Despite the presence of two National Leaguers on the board, it was the judgments of the forceful Johnson that usually prevailed. Ban, who was president of the American League until 1927, was without question the most powerful league executive in baseball history.

In their premier season of 1901 the American League had among its ranks baseball's most powerful hitter in Napoleon Lajoie. The twenty-five-year-old Rhode Island-born Frenchman came to the major leagues with the Philadelphia National League club in 1896, where he put in five bruising seasons at bat. When Connie Mack offered Nap nearly $6,000 a year to join his newly formed Philadelphia Athletics, Lajoie accepted.

To say that Connie got his money's worth in 1901 would be an understatement. Nap assaulted American League pitching all season long, taking the Triple Crown with 14 home runs, 125 runs batted in, and an olympian .422 batting average. In year one of the American League, Lajoie posted a batting average that remains unsurpassed, defying decades of assaults by sweet swingers like Ty Cobb, Joe Jackson, George Sisler, and Ted Williams. By all accounts, Nap was as smooth in the field as he was fearsome at bat. One word invariably came forth when they described him at work with the glove: graceful.

The game's number-one pitcher was also employed in the American League in 1901. Cy Young was thirty-four years old that year and had already won 285 of the 511 wins he registered before his retirement in 1911. His square handle was Denton True Young, the Cy being short for "Cyclone," a tag hung on him in tribute to his fast ball. And it must have been quite a quickie that Cy fired in, even at the age of thirty-four.

Working for the Boston Pilgrims—they weren't known as the Red Sox until a few years later—Cy logged a splendid 33–10 record, with league-leading figures in earned-run average (1.62), strikeouts (158), shutouts (5), and victories. He also knew where the plate was—walking just 37 batters in 371 innings, or one every ten innings.

In spite of Young's dazzling performance that year, the Pilgrims finished second, four games behind the league's first pennant winners, the Chicago White Sox. The White Sox, managed by Clark Griffith, who did his best managing from the mound, where he was 24–7, hotfooted themselves to the title with 280 stolen bases.

The American League gave its fans a pretty good pennant race in its maiden year, with third-place Detroit getting a look-see from 8½ games out. The Tiger lineup that year affords an interesting glimpse of the nicknames then in style. They had a Pop (Dillon), two Kids (Gleason and Elberfeld), two Docs (Casey and Nance), and one Ducky (Holmes). Homespun and flavorsome nicknames decorated rosters all around the league. Among the American League's cast of characters in that long-ago summer of fresh beginnings one found Dummy Hoy, Socks Seybold, Bones Ely, Snake Wiltse, Tacks Latimer, Crazy Schmidt, Candy LaChance, and Boileryard Clarke.

If there was any question about the new league's viability, it was dispelled once and for all in 1902. The attendance figures at the end of the season must have given the National League moguls a cold-water shock. The Americans drew a total of 2,228,000 to the Nationals' 1,684,000. In the four cities where the two leagues went head to head, Boston, Chicago, Philadelphia, and St. Louis, the new boys in town drew the greater numbers.

In 1902 Connie Mack won the first of his nine pennants, shepherding his Philadelphia Athletics in five games ahead of the St. Louis Browns. To legions of baseball fans who grew up in the 1930s, 1940s, and 1950s, Connie Mack was an old man of such erect and unassailable dignity that he seemed a natural patriarch who had been born looking like, well, Connie Mack. But even this symbol of distinguished perpetuity had been young once, was in fact not even Connie Mack but had originally been Cornelius McGillicuddy, born in East Brookfield, Massachusetts, in 1862. Connie had been a major-league catcher from 1886 to 1896, light of stick but shrewd of mind, and built like a fungo bat. He took over the Athletics in 1901 and reigned long and true, establishing a record for job stability astonishing for any profession, phenomenal for baseball. Virtually all of baseball's cherished records will no doubt be broken one day; but Connie Mack's fifty years at the helm of the Athletics will not be one of them. Being for much of the time owner of the club helped Connie's job security more than a little bit. Owner Mack and Manager Mack got along famously.

Connie passed with high marks the litmus test of any successful skipper: he had the admiration and respect of his men. Even when some of them had aged to the point where they began to look like Connie Mack, they recalled fondly the fair-minded treatment and fatherly concern they received from him. As a manager, he never donned a uniform, preferring to brainstorm in civvies from the dugout, a quirk that only added to his distinction. Although kindly and considerate, disdaining profanity, he could read a player out as thoroughly as McGraw; but Connie's style was to do it in the privacy of his office. He provided a very solid part of the foundation upon which Ban Johnson built his league.

It was a 136-game schedule in those first few years (the 154-game length didn't come in until 1904), and Connie's 83 victories were enough to take the pennant. Of those victories, more than half—44—were the work of two brilliant left-handers, George Edward (Rube) Waddell and Eddie Plank.

Mack's southpaw aces could not have been more unalike, both in personality and pitching style. Waddell was a big, lovable, childlike eccentric who loved to chase after fire engines and take days off during the summer to go fishing. He was a power pitcher, probably one of the fastest who ever lived, judging by his awesome strikeout totals in an era when the K's were harder to come by than they are today. He led American League pitchers in whiffs for six straight seasons, twice going over 300, with a high of 349 in 1904. In 1902, his first season in the American League, Rube was 24–7. Reminiscing 35 years later about his wayward ace, Connie conceded that Rube was probably his favorite among all the players he had managed. "Oh, he gave me fits," Connie said. "But he could pitch. That fellow could really pitch."

Waddell's antithesis in every conceivable way, Eddie Plank was Mack's other great left-hander. One of the first pitchers to work to spots, Plank threw his fast ball and curve with tireless precision. Year after year this reserved, poker-faced, somewhat enigmatic graduate of Gettysburg College gave Connie splendid service on the mound, winning over 20 games seven times and becoming the first pitcher working exclusively in the twentieth century to win 300 games.

In 1903 Waddell and Plank were again 20-game winners for the Athletics, but this time it wasn't enough as Boston, led by ageless Cy Young's 28 wins, easily outdistanced Connie's boys by 14½ games. Managing Boston and playing third base for them was Jimmy Collins, whom old-timers went to the grave swearing was the greatest glove ever to operate around the hot corner.

Nap Lajoie, playing with Cleveland, took another batting title, with a .355 average, but the man who might well have beat him out that year, Washington's thunderous-hitting Ed Delahanty, died in July in what remains an unexplained tragedy.

Big Ed, oldest of five brothers who played in the big time, had been an awesome buster in the National League through the 1890s, hitting over .400 three times. In 1902 he jumped from Philadelphia to the Washington club and hit a solid .376. In 1903 he was banging away at a .333 clip when he lost his life on July 2. Ed had left the team in Detroit and was returning east, reportedly to try and recover from illness. While riding a New York Central train across a bridge over Niagara Falls, Delahanty plunged from the train and was found below the falls a few days later. The mystery was never solved. Whether Ed had somehow fallen off while intoxicated—he was a heavy drinker—or committed suicide or was pitched off by some huskies after a brawl will never be known. He was thirty-five years old at the time of his death.

An agreement of lasting significance for baseball was made that August between the owners of the two clubs that were running away with their respective league pennants, Pittsburgh in the National League and Boston in the American. Pittsburgh's Barney Dreyfus and Boston's Henry Killilea agreed to match their clubs against each other in the fall in a best-five-out-of-nine series to determine the "world's champion." And thus the World Series was born, within a few years becoming America's most eagerly anticipated, followed, and discussed sporting event. (Only in 1904 was no series played, a cranky John McGraw unwilling to put his pennant-winning Giants on the field with an American League club.) Not only were the two leagues meeting on the same field of combat, but if there was any question left about the American League's legitimacy, it was dispelled by Boston's trimming of a very fine Pittsburgh club, five games to three.

Boston became the league's first repeater in 1904, but not until the final day of the season, edging out New York (then known as the "Highlanders"). The New Yorkers were in the race because of a truly heroic season-long pitching performance by their spitballing right-hander, "Happy" Jack Chesbro, who won an astounding 41 games, still the all-time record. Pitching with an arm that wouldn't quit, Chesbro started 51 games that year, completed 48, worked a titanic 455 innings, and won 41 and lost 12. But it all went down the drain with one errant toss.

This first of many New York-Boston nail-biters came down to the final day with Boston up by a game and a half and a doubleheader scheduled for New York's Hilltop Park. Boston needed one game to clinch; the Highlanders had to take both.

With Chesbro pitching against Boston's Bill Dineen, a mere 22-game winner, the opener went into the ninth tied 2–2. Lou Criger opened with a single, was sacrificed to second, and went to third on a ground out. Chesbro then uncorked history's most famous wild pitch, allowing Criger to score what proved to be the winning run, the pennant-winning run.

The Pilgrims won their flag primarily on pitching, getting 20-game seasons from Dineen and Jesse Tannehill, and 26 wins, including a perfect game from the thirty-seven-year-old Cy Young. Overall, the pitchers dominated the league in that 1904 season. There were ten 20-game winners (Mack's Waddell and Plank won 26 apiece), and the hurlers held the batters to a collective .249 batting average, a mark that made Nap Lajoie's league-leading .381 mark the more impressive.

Connie Mack's Athletics climbed to the top again in 1905, led by his southpaw aces Waddell (26–11) and Plank (25–12). This time they were abetted by right-hander Albert ("Chief") Bender, a canny, curve-balling Chippewa who won 16 games and was shortly to rise to such mound proficiency that he became Mack's "money pitcher."

Again it was a pitcher's banquet in the American League, to the extent that the leading batter, Cleveland's Elmer Flick, was able to win the batting title with a .306 bat-ting average, followed by New York's Willie Keeler, who popped just enough singles to hit .302, the league's only other .300 hitter. (The league's premier batsman, Nap Lajoie, was limited by an injury to just 65 games that season.) Overall, the league batted a noise-less .241. Mack's rugged first baseman Harry Davis was the home run leader with eight round trippers. The dead ball was never deader.

Slipping quietly into the league that season, however, was a slim, eighteen-year-old Georgian whom the Tigers purchased from Augusta in the Sally League in midseason. His name was Tyrus Raymond Cobb, and he was soon to see to it that .306 batting averages no longer qualified as league-leading figures.

He broke in modestly, batting just .240 in 41 games. He played for another 23 years and never deigned to bat so low again; in fact, he hit well over .300 in every one of those years and 16 times batted over .350, nine times over .380, and three times over .400.

He was one of a kind. Nothing like him had ever appeared on a baseball diamond before, nor has there been anything like him since. He became perhaps the greatest of all baseball players, the most feared, most hated, most respected, and most coldly and brutally efficient. He had a drive to excel that was called "frightening." Every time at bat was for Ty Cobb, a teammate said, "a crusade." To defend a base against an incoming Ty Cobb was to risk physical injury. One old-time third baseman said that Cobb's spikes "came at you like so many flashing knives," catapulted forward by the man's full fury.

A tautly muscled 6'1" 175 pounds, he possessed blinding speed, which he used audaciously and even recklessly on the base paths. A skilled bunter, a deadly place hitter, he was the unchallenged king of the dead-ball era.

Given his natural abilities and his fanatical competitive drive, Cobb would no doubt have dominated any era in which he played. Some people trace his near-psychotic personality to a family tragedy that occurred several years before he reached the big leagues. His father, said to be the only person Tyrus ever fully loved and respected, was shot to death by Ty's mother in what remains a rather murky case of mistaken identity. Mrs. Cobb shot her husband from her bedroom window, thinking, she later said, he was an intruder. Rumors that circulated at the time suggested that Cobb senior suspected his wife of being unfaithful and had planned an overnight trip in order to put his suspicions to the test, returning later that night and stealing up to the bedroom window. Whatever the truth of this, it is possible that his father's death had a deranging effect on the already temperamental and tempestuous youngster. Cobb once said that the reason he played so hard was because his father was "watching me."

In 1906 one of baseball's most memorable teams took the American League pennant. They were an aggregate that would never be confused with the 1927 Yankees. These were the Chicago White Sox of 1906, "the Hitless Wonders." With a feathery offense that batted an anemic .230 and hit just six home runs all season—both figures the lowest in the league that year—the White Sox still managed to come in three games ahead of New York and five ahead of Cleveland, a club that outhit the White Sox by 49 points, had three 20-game winners, and the league's lowest earned-run average. A late-season 19-game winning streak gave the White Sox the momentum to go on to take the pennant.

Managed by one of their outfielders with the splendid baseball name of Fielder Jones (that was his real name), the Sox had some fine pitching themselves, including a pair of winning lefties named Nick Altrock and Doc White, and two righties named Frank Owen and Ed Walsh, the latter a spitballer soon to emerge as one of the game's best pitchers. According to contemporaries, Big Ed's wet one was so lethal "it seemed to disintegrate on its

way to the plate."

For decade after decade the American League was destined to be the dominant factor in major-league baseball, for it seemed that whenever another ballplaying meteorite struck the earth he landed in the American League. Nothing typified this luck of the draw more than the 1907 season. With Ty Cobb beginning to ripen with the first of his twelve batting titles, three youngsters slipped unobtrusively into the league in 1907, each of them soon to make his name synonymous with all-time greatness.

Connie Mack brought to the major leagues a Columbia University product, left-handed-hitting infielder Eddie Collins. Originally a shortstop, the twenty-year-old Collins became in a few years a second baseman who soon rivaled and then surpassed the mighty Lajoie as the game's premier keystone performer. For decades Collins was the automatic choice as all-time second baseman, until finally the sheer weight of Rogers Hornsby's batting averages began blurring out Collins' intangibles.

Eddie's tangibles, however, were vivid enough. Across a 25-year career he batted .333, racked up 3,311 hits, stole 743 bases, and led in fielding nine times. One of the most intelligent men ever to play baseball, Collins was quiet and rock-steady, one of the least flamboyant of the great stars.

Getting into a handful of games for the Boston Red Sox in that 1907 season was a nineteen-year-old center fielder from Texas named Tristram Speaker. In a few years his play in center would become the standard for the position. He played what seemed a perilously shallow center field, to the extent that he made in his career four unassisted double plays, a record for an outfielder. Swift of foot, he possessed the instincts and reflexes of the outstanding athlete; few balls were hit over his head. His arm was powerful; his 35 assists in 1909 and again in 1912 remain the league record.

Along with his peerless defensive capacities, Speaker swung a sharp bat, collecting 3,515 lifetime hits, including an all-time high of 793 doubles, and finished with a .344 lifetime batting average, fourth highest among twentieth-century players with 1,000 or more games played. He remains the center fielder on many all-time teams, though of late he has been crowded here and there by Joe DiMaggio.

There is an informal way of gauging just how exquisite a ballplayer's skills were, beyond the impersonal revelations of the record books, and it comes from the testimony of their contemporaries. Men who played on the same field with Ty Cobb, Babe Ruth, Joe DiMaggio, Ted Williams, and a small handful of others recall these titans with pride and awe and reverence, bathing in reflected glory. Many of Tris Speaker's teammates and opponents bring that quality of memory to the talents of the man they called "Spoke" or "the Gray Eagle." Smokey Joe Wood, a 34-game winner for the Red Sox in 1912, would say seventy years later, at the age of ninety-two, that the thing he was proudest of in his major-league career was having roomed with Tris Speaker.

The third lightning bolt to strike the American League in 1907 was a nineteen-year-old right-handed pitcher named Walter Perry Johnson. This modest, soft-spoken native of Humboldt, Kansas, was to become the epitome of pitching power, the yardstick by which all future fast ballers were measured.

Johnson never pitched in the minor leagues. According to legend, he was spotted by a traveling salesman while pitching semi-pro ball in Idaho. The salesman wrote such glowing and persuasive letters to the Washington ball club that midway through the season a scout was dispatched, took one look at Johnson's astonishing fast ball, and signed the youngster for a $100 bonus and $350 a month for the rest of the season. Johnson made his debut against a hard-hitting Detroit club and, although losing 3–2, made a lasting impression on Ty Cobb. After watching the rookie warm up, Cobb turned to a teammate on the bench and said, "That busher throws the fastest pitch I've ever seen."

Fortunately for American League batters, Johnson was an uncommonly good-natured and gentle person. He refused to throw at opposing batters, nor would he even come close, fearing that with his lethal speed he might maim or kill someone. Once the canny Cobb realized this, he made it a practice to crowd the plate on Johnson, forcing the great fireballer to pitch away from him. Over his career Cobb batted against Johnson more frequently than against any other pitcher. In 245 times at bat, Ty batted .335 against the man considered by many to be baseball's number-one all-time pitcher.

It was Johnson's misfortune to work his entire 21-year career for a chronic loser. In ten of those years the Senators finished in the second division; only once, in 1918, did they ever come as close as four games to first place, until finally winning back-to-back pennants in 1924 and 1925.

Was he the fastest that ever lived? Probably. The grounds for this supposition are fairly sound when one realizes that the fast ball, propelled plateward with an easy, buggywhip sidearm motion, was the only pitch Walter threw. Outside of an occasional curve, which contemporaries said he telegraphed and was easy to hit, all he fired up to the plate were fast balls. "We knew damned well what was coming," said Roger Peckinpaugh, an outstanding shortstop who faced Walter many times. "But we still couldn't hit it."

In 1907–1909 the Detroit Tigers, led by young Ty Cobb, ran off three consecutive pennants. With his fires blazing higher and higher, Cobb won the first three of his nine consecutive batting titles, as well as leading in hits and runs batted in, in each of those seasons. Backing up Ty in the lineup was hard-hitting Sam Crawford (they were the only two Tigers to clear the .300 mark in those three pennant-winning years).

The Tigers received consistently strong pitching throughout their three pennant years from righties Wild Bill Donovan, George Mullin, Ed Willett, and Ed Summers, and lefty Ed Killian.

The Tigers had to scrap for each of their flags. In 1907 they nosed out the Athletics by 1½ games, in 1908 they edged Cleveland by just a half game, and in 1909 headed the A's by 3½.

The 1908 pennant race was one of the closest in history. The Indians were a half game out at the end and the White Sox just 1½. The gem of the season, one of the greatest pitched games in baseball history, took place on October 2 between the Indians and White Sox, both clubs locked in a tense three-way battle with the Tigers.

The opposing pitchers were Chicago's Ed Walsh, tireless, heroic, and lion-hearted that year in winning 40 games, pitching 464 innings, and posting a 1.42 earned-run average; and Cleveland's Addie Joss. (At career's end they would be 1–2 in lifetime earned-run average: Walsh with 1.82, Joss 1.88.) Joss, who did a complete spin on the mound before whirling around to whip in whistling fast balls and sharp curves, was one of the finest pitchers the game has ever known. No doubt his reputation would stand higher today if not for his untimely death from tubercular meningitis in 1911, two days after his thirty-first birthday.

With the pennant up for grabs that October afternoon, Walsh hurled his usual tight game, allowing one run on four hits while striking out 15. Joss, however, was perfect, literally. Addie saw 27 men and retired 27 in machine-gun order, pitching the league's second perfect game.

By the end of its first decade, the American League was more than solidly entrenched; it was superior to the National, outdrawing its older rival. And it would get better, winning

eight of the ten World Series played from 1910 through 1919. Among its incomparable array of stars were twenty-two-year-old Ty Cobb, twenty-two-year-old Eddie Collins, twenty-one-year-old Walter Johnson, and twenty-one-year-old Tris Speaker. And in a few years it would unveil the mightiest force ever to explode on a baseball diamond; the most awesome, charismatic, and captivating baseball player of them all—George Herman ("Babe") Ruth.

Iron Man McGinnity. Joe pitched in the American League for just a year and a half before jumping back to the National with the Giants in 1902.

Cy Young.

Nap Lajoie soon after joining the Philadelphia Athletics in 1901.

Bobby Wallace. He was known as "Mr. Shortstop," and soon after jumping to the Browns in 1902 his $6,000 per annum salary made him the game's highest paid player. He played in the big leagues for 25 years, 15 of them with the Browns.

Jimmy Collins.

Ed Delahanty.

George Stone, a left-handed-hitting outfielder who played for the Browns from 1905 through 1910. In 1906 he was the league's leading hitter, with a .358 batting average.

Wee Willie Keeler.

Sam Crawford, Detroit outfielder and one of the league's premier sluggers in the early decades of the century. Triples were his specialty—he led five times and had 312 lifetime, the all-time career high.

Jack Chesbro, a 41-game winner for New York in 1904.

Pitching for Detroit from 1903 through 1912, Wild Bill Donovan had his biggest year in 1907, when he was 25–4.

Bobby Wallace at bat in the early part of the century. Note that catchers were not yet wearing shin guards. Shin guards did not come into general use until around 1910.

Clark Griffith, a force in the American League for over a half century as player, manager, and owner of the Washington Senators.

Bill Bradley, Cleveland third baseman from 1901 through 1910. He batted .340 in 1902, his best year.

Ralph ("Socks") Seybold, an outfielder for the Athletics from 1901 through 1908. His 16 home runs in 1902 was the league record until Babe Ruth hit 29 in 1919.

Connie Mack.

Rube Waddell, for six consecutive years (1902–1907) the American League's strikeout leader.

After nine years in the National League, Monte Cross jumped to the Athletics in 1902 and played shortstop for Connie Mack until 1907.

Eddie Plank, first pitcher to win 300 games in the twentieth century. Lifetime record: 306–181.

Tully ("Topsy") Hartsel, one of Connie Mack's outfielders from 1902 through 1911. A sharp-eyed leadoff man, Topsy led the league in bases on balls five times.

Harry Bemis, Cleveland catcher from 1902 through 1910.

Nap Lajoie.

Patsy Dougherty, outfielder with Boston, New York, and Chicago from 1902 through 1911. He batted .342 in his rookie year with Boston, .331 a year later.

Bill Dinneen became an American League umpire after his pitching career was over. The right-hander was a 20-game winner for Boston in 1902, 1903, and 1904. He retired in 1909 with a 171–178 career mark.

Harry Davis, Connie Mack's bulwark first baseman during the first decade of the century. Harry led the league in home runs four straight years, 1904 through 1907, in runs batted in, 1905 and 1906.

Right-hander Long Tom Hughes was a 20-game winner for Boston in 1903. He spent the bulk of his career with Washington, retiring in 1913 with a 132–171 lifetime record.

After four hard-hitting seasons in the National League, outfielder Elmer Flick joined the Athletics in 1902, then was dealt to Cleveland, for whom he played until 1910. He won the batting title with a .306 average in 1905; he also led in triples in 1905, 1906, and 1907. Lifetime batting average: .315.

Wid Conroy, infielder-outfielder with New York and Washington from 1903 through 1911. Note the quality of Conroy's glove. That's what big leaguers used in those days.

Norman ("Kid") Elberfeld, shortstop for Detroit, New York, and Washington from 1901 through 1911.

Terry Turner played shortstop and then third base for Cleveland from 1904 through 1918. His high-water mark was .308 in 1912.

Lee Tannehill. Light of stick but sure of glove, Tannehill played third base for the White Sox from 1903 to 1912 despite a lifetime average of .220.

Ed Walsh. Big Ed has two distinctions: he was a 40-game winner in 1908, and in 1910 he led in earned-run average with 1.27 as well as games lost (20). Ed's White Sox teammates gave him many a sleepless night that year with a .211 collective batting average.

Right-hander Al Orth jumped to the American League with Washington in 1902 and later went on to the Yankees, for whom he won 25 games in 1906.

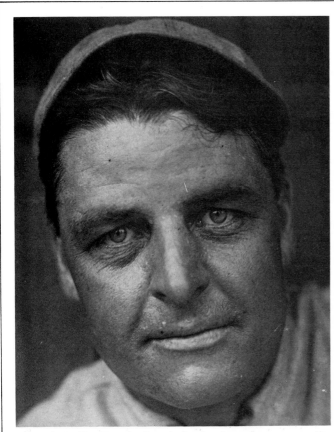

Right-hander Frank Smith had some fine years for the White Sox in the early days. In 1907 he was 23–11, in 1909, 24–17.

Charlie O'Leary, Detroit shortstop from 1904 to 1912. Charlie never stunned anybody with his hitting—his lifetime average is .226—but they say he was smooth in the field.

Herman ("Germany") Schaefer, second baseman for Detroit and Washington from 1905 through 1914. Normally a modest sticker, he went way over his head with a .334 average for Washington in 1911. He had a reputation for being a blithe spirit, and legend has it that one day, while he was on second base, he decided to liven up the proceedings by stealing first base.

Ty Cobb. At one time or another he led the league in everything, except making friends.

Nick Altrock, another White Sox ace who won 20 in 1904, 22 in 1905, 21 in 1906, then bit the dust with a sore arm.

Guy ("Doc") White, another White Sox winning pitcher early in the century. Doc jumped from the Phillies to join the Sox in 1903 and pitched for Chicago until 1913. In 1906 he was 18–6 with a league-leading 1.52 ERA; the following year he hit his peak with a 27–13 record. His lifetime record is 189–156.

This noble-looking gentleman in the high collar is Otto Hess, Cleveland left-hander, who was 20–17 in 1906.

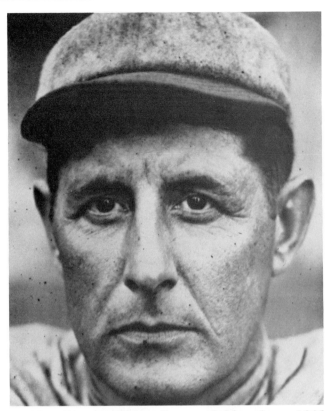

Fielder Jones, White Sox outfielder from 1901 through 1908; the last five years he was also manager. Jones jumped to the American League after five years with Brooklyn and in 1901 had his best year, when he batted .340.

Danny Hoffman, outfielder with the Athletics, Yankees, and Browns from 1903 through 1911.

Right-hander Bob Rhoads pitched for Cleveland from 1903 through 1909, with a 22–10 record in 1906 his best effort.

Addie Joss, Cleveland's ace from 1902 through 1910, the year before his death at the age of thirty-one. Four times a 20-game winner, he was 27–10 in 1907, 24–12 a year later. His overall record is 160–97, with 235 complete games in 261 starts. Only once in nine years did his earned-run average ever exceed 2.26; five times he averaged less than two runs per game, and in 1908 his league-leading ERA was 1.16.

Outfielder Davy Jones left the National League to join the Tigers in 1906, remaining with Detroit until 1912. Steady rather than spectacular, Davy was a .270 hitter.

Left-hander Ed Killian joined the Tiger staff in 1904 and a year later was 22–15. In 1907 he helped pitch the Tigers to their first pennant, with a 25–13 record. Lifetime he was 101–79.

Ed Summers broke in with a 24–12 record with the Tigers in 1908. The following year he helped Detroit to a third straight pennant, when he was 19–9. Arm trouble cut short his career and he retired after the 1912 season with a 68–45 record.

Jake Stahl, first baseman with the Red Sox, Senators, and Yankees from 1903 through 1913. He led the league with 10 home runs in 1910. Jake managed the Red Sox in 1912, when they won the pennant and World Series.

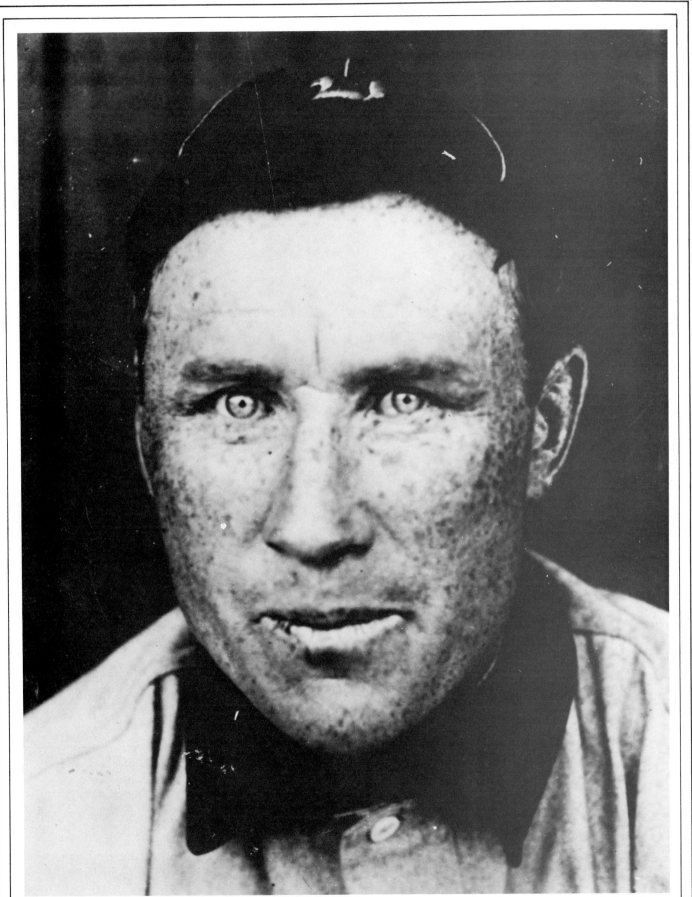

Formerly a star shortstop with the old Baltimore Orioles in the 1890s, Hughie Jennings managed the Tigers from 1907 through 1920.

George Mullin was Detroit's reigning ace throughout most of his career (1902–1913). Five times a 20-game winner, Mullin's peak season was 1909, when he was 29–8. His lifetime record is 212–181.

George Stovall, Cleveland first baseman from 1904 through 1911. A zealous competitor, George was known as "Firebrand."

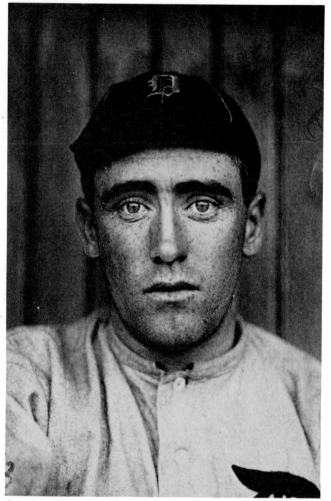

Right-hander Jimmy Dygert pitched for the Athletics from 1905 through 1910, with a 20–9 season in 1907 his best showing.

Owen ("Donie") Bush, Detroit's spark-plug short-stop from 1908 to 1921, finishing up with Washington in 1923. A .250 lifetime hitter, Bush led the league in bases on balls five times.

Ed Willett, another mainstay on the pitching staffs that helped Detroit win pennants in 1907–1909. Ed's best year was 1909, when he was 21–11. Lifetime he was 95–80.

Walter Johnson.

Joe Birmingham, Cleveland outfielder from 1906 through 1914. Joe, who managed the Indians from 1912 to 1915, batted .254 lifetime. As an outfielder, he was noted for the strength of his throwing arm.

This is Washington left-hander Ewart Gladstone ("Dixie") Walker, who had a brief, not very notable career with the Senators from 1909 through 1912. Walker's contribution to baseball came years later—his sons Fred (also known as Dixie) and Harry were outfielders who won National League batting crowns in the 1940s.

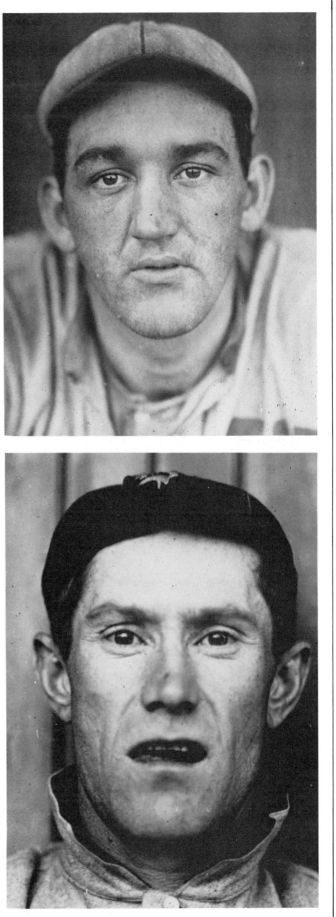

Hal Chase, the brilliant and controversial first baseman, considered the slickest glove of his time. He came up with the Yankees in 1905 and played for New York until traded to the White Sox in 1913. His best American League season came in 1906, when he batted .323. He won the National League batting crown while playing for Cincinnati in 1916. He was suspected of being a go-between for gamblers and the White Sox players who threw the 1919 World Series.

Jim Delahanty, brother of Ed and one of five Delahanty brothers to play in the big leagues. Jim, an infielder, played for four National League clubs before coming to the American League in 1907 with the Browns. He later played for Washington and Detroit, batting .339 for the Tigers in 1911. Lifetime he batted .283.

Eddie Collins.

More Than Equal

The Tigers' bid for a fourth consecutive pennant in 1910 was derailed by Connie Mack's Philadelphia Athletics. Detroit's pitching, superb the three previous years, slumped off, but even if it had not, it is doubtful that they could have touched the A's that year.

Mack had built shrewdly and well as he put his club together. Along with the veteran Harry Davis at first base, he had three talented youngsters in the infield—Eddie Collins at second, Jack Barry at short, and Frank Baker at third (two years later his home run heroics against the Giants in the World Series would earn this Maryland strongboy the nickname "Home Run"). In the outfield Connie had a couple of .300 hitters in Danny Murphy and Rube Oldring.

The A's were strong on the mound, the staff headed by 31-game winner Jack Coombs and 23-game winner Chief Bender. Between them, these two righties had a won-lost total of 54–14, accounting for more than half of the club's 102 victories—the first time an American League club had won over 100. The Athletics finished a healthy 14½ games ahead of second-place New York.

The dethroned Tigers, in third place, had little going for them that season outside of Ty Cobb's pursuit of a fourth straight batting title. Cobb got his title, with a .385 mark, but not before some end-of-the-season shenanigans that left a sour taste all around.

On the final day of the season Cobb had a comfortable 10-point lead over Nap Lajoie. Unwilling to risk losing the crown, Cobb took himself out of the lineup, while Lajoie had to play a doubleheader in St. Louis against the Browns, needing a barrage of hits to overtake Cobb. Adding a bit of spice to the season-long contest was a prize of an automobile offered to the champion by the Chalmers people.

By the 1910 season Cobb had achieved two distinctions; he was the league's greatest player and its most disliked. In some quarters he was flat-out hated. Included in this latter company was his own manager, Hughie Jennings, who said that Cobb was the greatest player in history but that he would love to trade him if he could get equal value. But nowhere in baseball was there equal value for Ty Cobb.

Lajoie, on the other hand, was one of the most admired players of the day. Consequently, the Browns' manager, Jack O'Connor, and one of his coaches, Harry Howell, cooked up a scheme to try and throw the crown to Lajoie. Installing a rookie named Red Corriden at third base, they instructed him to play back on the grass whenever Lajoie came to bat.

On his first at bat, Lajoie tripled. On subsequent times to the plate, however, he took note of Corriden playing far out of position and began dropping bunts. Nap, who was doing nothing wrong, simply exploiting a situation, wound up the day going 8 for 8. When the official tabulations were released, however, they showed Cobb as the leader, .385 to .384.

But the episode was not over. When Ban Johnson heard about the skulduggery engineered by O'Connor and Howell, he was infuriated. The league president ordered both conspirators bounced out of the American League and neither ever appeared on a big-league diamond again. The Chalmers people, impressed by Lajoie's last-ditch effort, ended up giving cars to both Ty and Nap.

This probably was not an isolated bit of monkey business. It is widely suspected that at the time there was a good deal of betting done on games by players, as well as games being thrown. Players like New York's superb first baseman Hal Chase (his skipper, Frank Chance, said Hal had a "corkscrew mind") openly consorted with gamblers, and some of Chase's misplays in the field were looked upon with suspicion by teammates. Unsavory activities were simmering in baseball, and by the end of the decade it would all explode and hit the fan—both the proverbial one and the one in the grandstands—with full force.

Connie Mack had another romp in 1911, finishing 13½ games ahead of Detroit, despite not taking over first place until August 4. Cobb won another batting title with his greatest season ever, hitting .420, backed by Sam Crawford's .378. The two Tiger outfielders combined for 465 hits. But Detroit ran up against what Mack later considered the greatest of all his teams, a club highlighted by what Connie described in then-grandiose terms as his "hundred-thousand-dollar infield." This inner defense consisted of Collins, Barry, Baker, and newcomer John ("Stuffy") McInnis at first base.

With Collins leading the way with a .365 average, the Athletics studded their lineup with five .300 hitters, giving the team a .296 batting mark, a new high for the league. This ball-pounding made things a bit easier for Mack's fine mound staff. Coombs followed his 31-game season with 28 wins, the ageless Plank won 22, and Bender 17.

The season also saw the introduction by the Cleveland Indians of the man called by many "the greatest natural hitter who ever lived." His name was Joe Jackson and they called him "Shoeless" for allegedly having played sans footwear in the pastures of his native South Carolina. The good-natured, semiliterate twenty-one-year-old with the flawless left-handed swing had a Rookie-of-the-Century season—233 hits, including 45 doubles, 19 triples, and a .408 batting average. But Ty Cobb welcomed the young man to the American League by edging him out in each department. Joe returned to South Carolina that winter scratching his head, wondering what a fellow had to do.

In 1912 the biggest name in baseball belonged, not to Ty Cobb or Walter Johnson or Christy Mathewson or Honus Wagner, but to a baby-faced twenty-two-year-old right-hander on the Boston Red Sox named Smokey Joe Wood. The year before, the flame-throwing youngster was 23–17, a season that left him poised at the very brink of greatness. In 1912 he went over the brink, putting together what remains a Mount Everest of a season for pitchers.

With the Red Sox celebrating the opening of their new ball yard, Fenway Park, Wood put on a season-long celebration of his own, winning 34 and losing just 5, fanning 258 and hurling 10 shutouts (he also batted .290; the kid was a piece of work).

Wood had but one mound rival that year—Walter Johnson. In full glory now, Walter was 32–12, with 303 strikeouts and a 1.39 earned-run average. Along the way he rang up 16 straight wins, rubbing out Jack Chesbro's previous record of 14 in a row, set in 1904. But Johnson had no sooner applied the varnish to his new mark than he looked over his shoulder to see young Wood steaming along the same tracks. Joe had 13 in a row when Washington came to Fenway Park on September 6, 1912. Wood, a zealous competitor, had his eye fixed on the record. He needed 3 more. But on that day he found himself matched against the record holder himself—Walter Johnson.

If ever there was a dream match-up, this was it. It was Dempsey and Louis in spiked shoes, ready to fire an afternoon's worth of the most blazing fast balls anyone had ever seen. The analogy is not too farfetched. According to Wood, "The newspapers publicized us like prizefighters: giving statistics comparing our height, weight, biceps, triceps, arm span, and whatnot. The Champion, Walter Johnson, versus the Challenger, Joe Wood."

Fenway Park overflowed that day, with fans standing behind outfield ropes. And they saw what they came to see. Appropriately for a pitching match made in heaven, it was a 1–0 game, with young Wood coming up the winner. The Boston run scored in the sixth inning on back-to-back doubles by Tris Speaker and Duffy Lewis.

Wood went on to win his next two decisions before losing, leaving him tied for the record with Johnson, 16 consecutive victories each, set in 1912.

Guided by Wood's rocket arm and Speaker's .383 bat, the Red Sox broke the Athletics' two-year-old record with 105 wins on their way to the pennant.

The season saw another batting crown for Cobb, Ty pinking the ball for a .410 average this time. Joe Jackson, in his second full season, batted .395 and still wasn't close to a title. First .408, then .395, and still no cigar. A fellow could get discouraged.

In the spring of 1913 the comet named Joe Wood suddenly and sadly ceased to illuminate the baseball skies. Boston's twenty-three-year-old fireballer hurt his arm in spring training and just like that, as if in illustration of fate's caprices or to show how truly gossamer the sinews that separate greatness from mediocrity, Joe Wood was no longer a star. He pitched for the Red Sox for another three years, his arm sore and painful, but with enough hop left on his fast ball to log a 15–5 record in 1915 and a league-leading 1.49 earned-run average.

If Joe Wood's was the career that never was, then Walter Johnson's was the career that became the most captivating of any pitcher's, and never more so than in 1913. By now they were calling him "the Big Train," in comparison with the era's idea of unimaginable speed. Walter had his greatest year in 1913, thus by definition the greatest any pitcher ever enjoyed. He was 36–7, leading the league in wins, earned-run average (1.09), complete games (30), innings pitched (346), strikeouts (243), and shutouts (12). For more than a month, from April 10 to May 14, he allowed no runs, pitching 55⅔ scoreless innings, a record that stood until 1968, when Don Drysdale spun out 58 runless frames in a row. In his 346 fast-balling innings, Johnson walked just 38. (This was an example of the famous control for which churchgoing American League batters gave thanks every Sunday.)

Walter also relieved a dozen times that season, picking up seven wins against no losses coming out of the bullpen. It must have been quite a disheartening sight for opposing hitters to watch long-armed Walter Johnson walking out of the pen in the late innings of a close game, especially with the shadows beginning to fall.

Despite Walter's titanic season, the best Washington could do was finish second to the Athletics, 6½ games behind. Cobb won a seventh straight batting title, with a .390 average, with Joe Jackson second again for the third year in a row, with a .373 mark. By now Joe must have been philosophical about the whole thing.

Connie Mack made it four out of five in 1914, finishing 8½ in front of a Red Sox team primed now to forge a small dynasty of its own. The stars remained firmly in place in the American League firmament, with Cobb leading again with .368, despite losing a third of a season with broken ribs, and Walter Johnson winning 28 and leading his pitching colleagues in everything except cusswords, which he never used. Despite a 1.71 ERA, Walter came within one of also leading in losses—he dropped 18—because of his team's feeble attack.

In July 1914 the Red Sox paid the Baltimore Orioles of the International League $25,000 for three players, catcher Ben Egan and pitchers Ernie Shore and George Herman ("Babe") Ruth. Ruth, a nineteen-year-old left-hander, was in his first year of professional ball. At the end of the International League season he showed a 22–9 record and the Red Sox brought him up. They started him three times and he did well, winning two and losing one. At the plate he batted .200, going 2 for 10, one of his hits a double. Red Sox Manager Bill Carrigan let him pinch-hit once. "He looked like he might be handy with a bat," the skipper said. Thus did Babe Ruth launch the mightiest of all baseball careers and one of the most mythological of American lives.

In the spring of 1914 war broke out in Europe. Not to be outdone, major-league baseball found itself in a fracas of its own at the same time. The peace that had existed for the decade since the National League sighed and gave its mixed blessing to the American was broken by a pretender that called itself the Federal League.

Naturally the two established major leagues were outraged by the intruder. Ban Johnson called the newcomers exactly the same things he himself had been called 13 years earlier by the National League, but as an autocrat Ban was immune to feelings of irony or accusations of hypocrisy.

The Federal League, however, was destined to be considerably less successful than Ban and his cohorts had been in raiding the big-league rosters. There were some defections, most of them from the National League. The few American League "names" who displayed human frailty when confronted by bigger money included Detroit pitcher George Mullin and Philadelphia outfielder Danny Murphy, both over the hill. In 1915 the A's lost ace pitcher Chief Bender and the veteran Eddie Plank.

But it was a losing battle for the Feds. Unable to attract major stars, they were doomed. They did make overtures to Cobb, Speaker, and Johnson, but those worthies refused to succumb, their resolve helped along by substantial salary increases. Cobb reportedly got a hike from $12,000 a year to $20,000. When the Federal League Chicago club offered Walter Johnson $16,000, Walter's boss, the parsimonious Clark Griffith, was not only furious but also felt faint at the thought of meeting the figure (Walter was being paid considerably less). To make matters worse, the Feds were also offering Walter a $10,000 signing bonus, and it was this that began straining his loyalty. Unable to ante up the extra ten grand with which to keep his ace, the canny Griffith turned to his old pal Charlie Comiskey, owner of the Chicago White Sox. Griff painted a bleak picture for Charlie of Walter pitching for the new club in Chicago. The thought of the game's biggest drawing card working for his new crosstown rivals sent Charlie unhappily to his checkbook. It was Comiskey's ten grand that kept Johnson in the league.

Without big-name stars, the Feds were out of luck. They kept their act going for two years and then folded their tents. At the end they were charging ten cents a ticket, but the fans felt they weren't worth even that much.

The Federal League threat to his stars, plus financial pressures, forced Connie Mack to break up what had been up to that point the greatest team in American League history. With Plank and Bender already gone, Connie sold Eddie Collins to the White Sox, Jack Barry and fine young left-hander Herb Pennock to the Red Sox, right-hander Bob Shawkey to the Yankees, and released Jack Coombs. In addition, Frank Baker retired to run his Maryland farm (he came back with the Yankees a year later).

With this abrupt divestment of his stars, Connie Mack took the elevator down to the cellar, where he would remain for seven consecutive years.

It was too bad Mack could not keep his team intact, for there would surely have been some blistering pennant races with the powerful young Boston club.

The Red Sox took three pennants from 1915 to 1918, losing out only in 1917 to the White Sox. These Red Sox teams were splendidly balanced aggregations, featuring some of the strongest pitching staffs of all time; an outfield of Tris Speaker in center, Duffy Lewis in left, and Harry Hooper in right that remains

legendary for its defensive abilities; and a solid if unspectacular infield. The outfield was broken up in April 1916 when Speaker was dealt to Cleveland for having had the temerity to ask for a $15,000 salary. (Tris had a fine season for Cleveland in 1916, his .386 batting average leading the league and ending Cobb's string of nine straight titles.)

Among the outstanding Red Sox pitchers during those World War I championship seasons were righties George ("Rube") Foster, Carl Mays, and Ernie Shore; and left-handers Hubert ("Dutch") Leonard and Babe Ruth. In his first full season the twenty-year-old moon-faced Ruth was 18–6, with a 2.44 ERA. He also batted .315 and hit four home runs. A year later he was the ace, with a 23–12 mark and league-leading figures in ERA (1.75) and shutouts (9). In 1917 he was 24–13, with a 2.02 ERA, not to mention a .325 batting average. The colossus was clearly beginning to rise.

He was by now the league's premier lefty, but in 1918 Red Sox Manager Ed Barrow began to curtail his young star's pitching. Ruth started only 19 games that year, posting a 13–7 mark, appearing in 59 games in the outfield and 13 at first base. Clearly, Barrow valued the youngster's bat more than he did his arm. Ruth batted .300 that year and tied for the league lead in home runs with 11, the first of 12 home run titles he either took or tied for.

In 1919 Ruth played 111 games in the outfield and started but 15 on the mound. His pitching days were just about over now, and with good reason—he set a new home run record with an astonishing 29, breaking Socks Seybold's 1902 mark of 16 with plenty to spare. He also led in runs batted in with 114 and set a new record for slugging average with .657.

In spite of Ruth's booming bat, the Red Sox finished fifth. The winners in 1919 were the Chicago White Sox, a truly outstanding ball club—when they felt like playing. This was the team that threw the World Series to Cincinnati that fall, becoming to baseball history what Benedict Arnold is to American history.

Apparently this club did not lose its moral perspective all of a sudden that October. Roger Peckinpaugh, then a star shortstop for the Yankees, recalled the 1919 White Sox years later. "You just never knew when they were going to go out there and beat your brains out or roll over and play dead. Somebody was betting on those games, that's a cinch. When they wanted to play, you had a hard time beating them, that's how good they were."

The White Sox won the pennant by 3½ games over Cleveland. The stars of the club were Eddie Collins (true blue all the way; no would-be fixer would have dared approach him); Shoeless Joe Jackson, obtained from Cleveland in 1915; first baseman Chick Gandil; third baseman Buck Weaver; shortstop Swede Risberg; catcher Ray Schalk; and center fielder Happy Felsch. On the mound the White Sox had spitballing right-hander Eddie Cicotte (29–7) and lefty Claude Williams (23–11).

Eight members of the squad were involved in the series fix—Jackson, Weaver, Gandil, Risberg, Cicotte, Williams, Felsch, and utility infielder Fred McMullin. McMullin was little more than a guilty bystander, since his series appearances were limited to a couple of pinch-hitting roles. Of the eight, only Weaver did not actually participate in the monkeyshines. Buck's trouble derived from having known about the fix and keeping mum, an honorable course perhaps but chancy.

Despite rumors and mutterings, the lid did not come off until a year later, in September 1920, right at the tail end of a red-hot pennant chase between the White Sox, Indians, and Yankees.

There is reason to believe that White Sox owner Charles Comiskey had been advised that his team had thrown the series. But Charlie refused to believe it or, if he did believe, chose to do nothing about it. By September 1920, the rumors had become irrepressible. Some of the gamblers had spoken to newspapermen about the series. Ban Johnson, on the outs with Comiskey for some years, began pressing for a full and vigorous investigation.

A grand jury was convened in Chicago and before it Cicotte and Jackson confessed, implicating their guilty teammates.

The case followed a curious course. When it came to trial in June 1921, the players were acquitted by a jury that sympathized with them because none of the gamblers involved had been brought to the bar. The last word, however, and now the supreme word, came from baseball's brand-new commissioner, Judge Kenesaw Mountain Landis.

Landis, a federal judge, had been hired by the game's panicky owners to bring law and order to a game in which they feared the public was losing confidence. Landis, whose stern features suggested Old Testament authority and inflexible integrity—he looked and acted like a third-rate thespian impersonating a judge—became baseball's unforgiving arbiter of its integrity. Despite the jury's acquittal of the eight dubious White Sox players, the judge pitched them out of the game forever. A frown from the judge was almost as good as getting the rope.

It was a tense year in baseball, that year of 1920. Along with the breaking scandal, the game's greatest tragedy occurred on August 16 in a New York-Cleveland game at the Polo Grounds (then the home field of the Yankees). Yankee pitcher Carl Mays, a tough-minded submarine baller, fired an inside fast ball that struck Cleveland shortstop Ray Chapman in the head. Chapman collapsed at home plate and died the next day in a New York hospital without ever having regained consciousness. He remains the only on-the-field fatality in major-league history.

The tragedy might have shattered most pitchers, but Carl Mays was cold and tough. A teammate said that a year later in spring training Mays was lecturing young pitchers on the importance of working hitters inside, not to let them crowd the plate.

But while all of that was going on, the sordid and the tragic, the loss of trust and the shattering of careers and the death of a player, there had been turned loose in the universe of baseball a force so gargantuan and exciting and breathtaking, so obviously one of a kind, that supposedly disillusioned American League fans were storming the turnstiles in record numbers to see it in action.

John ("Stuffy") McInnis, first baseman on Connie Mack's "hundred-thousand-dollar infield." He joined the A's in 1909 and became a regular two years later. He was traded to the Red Sox in 1918 and then to Cleveland in 1922, playing there one year, after which he was traded to the National League, retiring in 1927. Steady as an April shower, McInnis only once batted under .290 in his career, going over .300 eleven times, with .327 his high in 1912. His lifetime average is .308.

Jack Barry, shortstop on Connie Mack's famous infield. Jack played for the A's from 1908 to 1915, when he was traded to Boston, for whom he played until 1919.

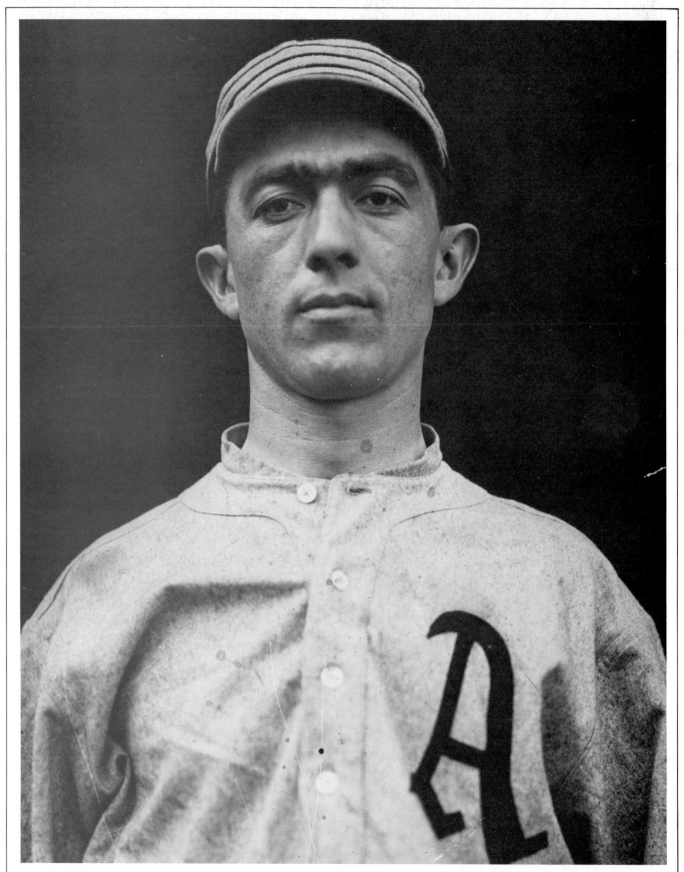

Frank ("Home Run") Baker, the muscleman on Mack's four pennant winners. He led four times in home runs, twice in runs batted in. In 1912 he batted .347, his personal high. He played from 1908 through 1922, dividing his time between the Athletics and Yankees. Lifetime batting average: .307.

Amos Strunk. He joined the A's in 1908 and had a 17-year career roaming through American League outfields. After leaving the A's in 1917 he played for Boston and Chicago.

Ira Thomas, a catcher for the Athletics from 1909 through 1915.

One of Connie Mack's stalwarts from 1902 through 1913, Danny Murphy came up as a second baseman, then moved to the outfield to make room for Collins. He batted .329 for Connie's 1911 pennant winners and .288 lifetime.

Rube Oldring, another member of Connie Mack's pre-World War I four-time pennant winners. An out-fielder, Rube was employed by Connie from 1906 through 1916.

The third outfielder on the team Mack called his greatest ever, the 1911 A's, had the resounding name of Bristol Robotham Lord. Bris Lord joined the A's in 1905, was exiled to Cleveland for a year and a half, and was reacquired by Mack in time to play on the 1911 club. Bris batted .310 that year, his best average, inspired, apparently, by the greatness around him. He left the big leagues in 1913.

Chief Bender, Connie Mack's curve-balling money pitcher. The Chief worked in Connie's vineyard from 1903 through 1914, when he jumped to the Federal League. His top year was 1910, when he was 23–5. Lifetime he was 206–112.

This rugged face belongs to Harry ("Cy") Morgan, who pitched for the Browns, Red Sox, and Athletics from 1903 through 1912. He was 18–11 for Mack in 1910 and 15–7 the next year but was overshadowed on a staff that included Plank, Bender, and Coombs. A right-hander, Cy was 76–75 lifetime.

Right-hander Jack Coombs, Connie Mack's ace in 1910 and 1911, when Colby Jack was 31–9 and 28–12. He was 20–10 in 1912, but then injuries cut him down and he drifted into the National League. Lifetime record: 158–111.

Third baseman Jimmy Austin came up with the Yankees in 1909 but played the bulk of his career with the Browns, being their regular third sacker until 1920.

Russ Ford had a sensational rookie year for the Yankees in 1910, with a 26–6 record and 1.65 ERA. He was 21–11 the next year, but after that he began turning in losing records. By 1914 he was out of the league.

Harry Lord, third baseman for the Red Sox and White Sox from 1907 through 1914. Harry's big year was 1911, when he batted .321 for the White Sox.

Russell ("Lena") Blackburne, light-hitting infielder for the White Sox around the time of World War I.

Clyde ("Deerfoot") Milan, Washington outfielder from 1907 through 1922. He was one of the league's premier rabbits in his heyday, stealing 88 bases in 1912 and 75 the next year. His career average is .285.

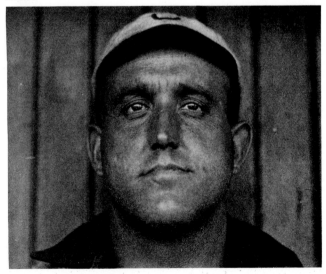

Cy Falkenberg, right-hander for Washington and Cleveland from 1905 through 1913. Cy's best year was 1913, when he was 23–10, after which he jumped to the Federal League.

This robust-looking gentleman is Irving Young, a left-handed pitcher who was called "Young Cy" and "Cy the Second" when he came into the National League with Boston in 1905. Irv did all right, but he remained Irv the First rather than Cy the Second. He joined the White Sox in 1910, pitched with modest distinction for two years, and then left the big leagues.

Right-hander Carroll ("Boardwalk") Brown, pitcher for Connie Mack from 1911 to 1914, finishing up with the Yankees a year later. Boardwalk helped Connie to a pennant in 1913, with a 17–11 record.

Harry Krause. A sore arm prevented this young southpaw from what might have been a brilliant career. Joining the Athletics in 1909, Harry was 18–8 with a scintillating league-leading ERA of 1.39. He was just twenty-two years old. An arm injury the following year turned him into a .500 pitcher and by 1913 he was gone.

Shoeless Joe Jackson with the Cleveland Indians in 1910.

Jack Lapp, back-up catcher for the Athletics from 1908 through 1915.

Dodger fans remember him as the kindly old gentleman who skippered their team to pennants in 1947 and 1949 but before that Burt Shotton was a hotfooting outfielder with the St. Louis Browns from 1909 to 1917. He later played for the Senators and Cardinals before retiring in 1923. Burt never broke down any fences, but he did end up with a lifetime batting average of .270.

Bob Groom broke in with the Senators in 1909 with a 6–26 record. He began improving, however, and in 1912 was 24–13, his best season. He later pitched for the Browns and Indians, retiring in 1918 with a 96–122 record.

Catcher Eddie Ainsmith, who caught Walter Johnson's fast ones from 1910 through 1918.

Walter Johnson in 1912.

Smoky Joe Wood in 1912.

Hugh Bedient broke in with the Red Sox in 1912 with a 20–9 record. He was 16–14 the next year, then 9–12. He pitched in the Federal League in 1915 and then, at the age of twenty-six, left the scene.

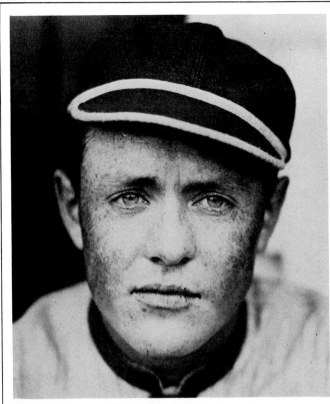

Eddie Foster, Washington's regular third baseman from 1912 through 1919. He later played for the Red Sox and Browns, retiring in 1923 with a batting average of .264.

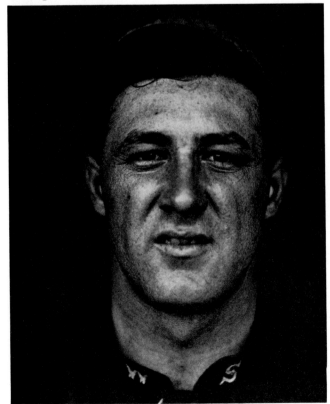

Frank ("Ping") Bodie, outfielder with the White Sox, Athletics, and Yankees from 1911 to 1921.

Thomas ("Buck") O'Brien joined the Red Sox at the end of the 1911 season, helped pitch them to a pennant the next year with a 19–13 record, then hurt his arm and was gone the next year.

Ray Collins was the only left-hander on Boston's fine pennant-winning 1912 staff. Ray was 15–8 that year, then turned in seasons of 20–8 and 20–13 before bowing out with a bad arm. He pitched for the Red Sox from 1909 through 1915.

Charley ("Sea Lion") Hall pitched for the Red Sox from 1909 through 1913. His best showing was a 15–8 record in the 1912 pennant year.

Del Pratt, second baseman for the Browns, Yankees, Red Sox, and Tigers from 1912 through 1924. The league's RBI leader in 1916 with 103, Del batted over .300 six times and finished up with a .292 lifetime.

Catcher Steve O'Neill, one of four brothers to play big-league ball. Steve caught for the Indians from 1911 through 1923, then briefly for the Red Sox, Yankees, and Browns, retiring in 1928. He caught the full season for Cleveland's 1920 pennant winners, batting .321. Lifetime he was a .263 hitter. He later managed the Indians, Tigers, Red Sox, and Phillies.

Jack Graney, Cleveland outfielder from 1908 through 1922. Lifetime average: .250.

Jim Scott, White Sox right-hander from 1909 through 1917. Jim's best was a 24–11 record in 1917. He retired with a career mark of 111–113.

John ("Shano") Collins, outfielder with the White Sox from 1910 through 1920 and with the Red Sox through 1925. Lifetime average: .264.

George ("Hooks") Dauss, Detroit's solid pitcher from 1912 through 1926. Three times a 20-game winner, his top year was 1915, when he was 24–13. Lifetime he was 221–183.

Right-hander Bob Shawkey came up with the Athletics in 1913. Sold to New York in 1915, he immediately became a Yankee ace, winning 23 games in
1916. He won 20 on the nose for the Yanks in 1919,
1920, and 1922. He retired in 1927 with a 198–150
lifetime record. He managed the Yankees in 1930.

Wally Schang caught in the American League for 19
years, from 1913 to 1931. He came up with the Athletics and later played for the Red Sox, Yankees,
Browns, and Tigers. Six times a .300 hitter, his
peak was .330 for the Browns in 1926. Lifetime
average: .284.

Bullet Joe Bush had a long big-league career, from
1912 through 1928. The hard-throwing righty came
up with the Athletics, was dealt to the Red Sox in
1918 and then to the Yankees in 1921, when he had
his best year, 26–7, his only 20-game season. He
later pitched for the Browns and Senators before
going to the National League. His lifetime record
reads 196–181.

Herb Pennock, shown here in his rookie year with the Athletics, 1912, when he was eighteen years old. After an 11–4 year in 1914, he was dealt to the Red Sox, for whom he pitched until 1922, when he was traded to the Yankees. Herb was 19–6 in 1923, 21–9 the following year. In 1926 he was 23–11, followed by seasons of 19–8 and 17–6. He pitched in the American League for 22 years, retiring in 1934 with a 241–162 record.

After a nondescript career in the National League, left-hander Harry Coveleski joined the Tigers in 1914 and ran off years of 21–13, 22–13, and 22–11. He hurt his arm in 1917 and a year later was out of the big leagues.

Jack Fournier, first baseman with the White Sox from 1912 to 1917. Jack batted .311 in 1914, .322 a year later. Troubled by a leaky glove, he went to the National League, where he had a number of heavy-hitting seasons. Lifetime average: .313.

Fritz Maisel, Yankee third baseman from 1913 to 1917. He didn't hit for high average, but he made up for it on the base paths. He led the league with 74 stolen bases in 1914, still the Yankee team record.

Ray Caldwell as a Yankee rookie in 1910. The smooth-working right-hander pitched for New York until 1919, when he was traded to Boston, who promptly traded him to Cleveland. Ray was 20–10 as he helped the Indians to their first pennant in 1920. Lifetime he was 134–120.

Bill ("Rough") Carrigan. Bill caught for the Red Sox from 1906 through 1916, ending with a modest .257 lifetime average. It was as a manager, however, that Bill made his mark. Taking over in 1913, he managed until 1916, winning pennants in 1915 and 1916. He then retired to his home in Maine at the age of thirty-three, returning to take over the team again for three years in 1927. He was immensely popular with his players.

Tris Speaker in 1912.

George ("Duffy") Lewis, left fielder on the 1912 Red Sox pennant winners. Duffy had a reputation as a clutch hitter as well as being a peerless outfielder. He was with the Red Sox from 1910 through 1917, then was traded to the Yankees. He retired with the Washington Senators in 1921. His career average is .284.

Boston Red Sox southpaw Babe Ruth in 1915.

Harry Hooper, right fielder on the famed Lewis-Speaker-Hooper outfield. Harry was with the Red Sox from 1909 through 1920, then with the White Sox until 1925. He batted over .300 five times, his high .328 in 1924. Lifetime he batted .281.

Clarence ("Tilly") Walker, outfielder with Washington, St. Louis, Boston, and Philadelphia in the American League from 1911 through 1923. With the A's in 1918 Tilly led with 11 home runs (tying Babe Ruth). In 1922, the year before he retired, Tilly popped 37 homers, second to Ken Williams' 39. Lifetime batting average: .281.

Ernie Shore, Red Sox right-hander from 1914 through 1917. After a year in the service he was traded to the Yankees, retiring after the 1920 season. Ernie's best year was 1915, when he was 18–8 with a 1.64 ERA. In 1917 he pitched one of baseball's rare perfect games. Ruth started the game for Boston, walked the first batter, and was then ejected for arguing with the umpire. Shore took over, and after the man on first was caught stealing, Ernie retired the next 26 men in order. After some heavy thinking, the lords of baseball decided to credit Shore with a perfect game. For his injury-shortened career Shore was 63–42.

Hubert ("Dutch") Leonard. Dutch, a southpaw, joined the Red Sox in 1913. He had his best year in 1914, when he was 18–5 with a 1.01 ERA, lowest in big-league history. He was traded to Detroit in 1919 and pitched for them until 1925. Lifetime he was 138–113.

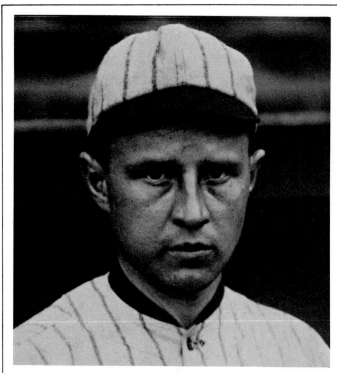

Harry ("Nemo") Leibold. He played in the American League for 13 years, from 1913 through 1925, putting in time with Cleveland, Chicago, Boston, and Washington. A member of the 1919 White Sox, Nemo had nothing to do with any of the funny business. He was a .266 lifetime hitter.

Ray Schalk, White Sox catcher from 1912 to 1928. Ray, who batted only .253, was regarded as one of the finest receivers of his era, with defensive skills good enough to get him voted into the Hall of Fame.

Bobby Veach, hard-hitting Detroit outfielder from 1912 through 1923. Bobby cleared the .300 mark eight times, with a high of .355 in 1919. Lifetime he batted .310.

Some players break in with a bang; right-hander Guy Morton broke in with a whimper, losing his first 13 decisions for Cleveland in his rookie year, 1914. Guy soon turned it around, however, and pitched for the Indians until 1924, when he retired with a 97–88 lifetime record.

St. Louis Browns left-hander Ernie Koob. Ernie pitched for the Browns from 1915 to 1919 with no great distinction (he was 23–30 lifetime), except for a couple of days in May 1917. On May 5 he tossed a no-hitter against the White Sox; the next day teammate Bob Groom did the same thing to the same club, the only time pitchers on the same team have thrown back-to-back no-hitters.

Joe Harris, outfielder-first baseman. Joe came up with the Indians in 1917 and later played for Boston and Washington before moving to the National League. Wherever he played, he hit, ending with a lifetime average of .317.

Charles Comiskey.

John ("Doc") Lavan, shortstop with the Browns and Senators during the World War I era. He later played for the Cardinals, retiring in 1924 after a 12-year big-league career, during which he averaged .245.

Eddie Cicotte pitched for the Red Sox from 1908 until 1912, when he was traded to the White Sox, where he found fame and infamy. He was 28–12 for Chicago in 1917 and 29–7 in 1919. Lifetime he was 210–148.

The talented Claude ("Lefty") Williams of the 1919 White Sox. He came up with Detroit in 1913 and joined the White Sox in 1917. After several winning seasons he was 23–11 in 1919 and 22–14 in 1920, when he was suspended that September. Only twenty-seven years old when he was barred from baseball, Williams left behind an 82–48 lifetime record and the wreckage of a potentially fine career.

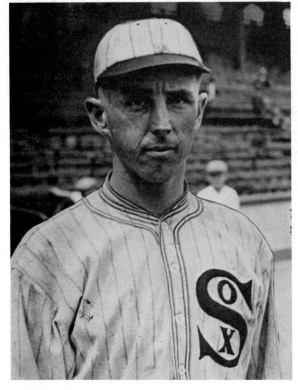

Third baseman George ("Buck") Weaver of the 1919 White Sox. Innocent of wrongdoing but guilty of knowing about it and saying nothing, Buck got the boot with his teammates. With the Sox since 1912, Buck was having by far his best year, when the roof caved in, in September 1920, batting .333 with 210 base hits. Overall he was a .272 sticker.

Oscar ("Happy") Felsch, White Sox center fielder on the 1919 club. With the team since 1915, Happy was having his best year in 1920 when things caught up to him that September, batting .338. He left behind a .293 lifetime average.

Charles ("Swede") Risberg, White Sox shortstop from 1917 to 1920, when he got the gate. Only twenty-six years old at the time, Swede left behind a .243 average.

Shoeless Joe Jackson. Lifetime batting average: .356.

Charles ("Chick") Gandil, first baseman on the 1919 White Sox and alleged by some the ringleader of the group involved in the scandal. A good if not spectacular ballplayer, Gandil came to the big leagues with the White Sox in 1910, played subsequently with Washington and Cleveland before being dealt back to the White Sox in 1917. His best year was 1913, when he batted .318 for Washington. He batted .277 for his nine big-league seasons.

Fred McMullin, utility infielder on the 1919 White Sox. Fred, who was with the White Sox from 1916 to 1920, filled in mostly at third base and hit like a utility infielder—his lifetime average was .256.

Dickie Kerr, one of the untainted. He pitched for the White Sox from 1919 through 1921, logging records of 13–7, 21–9, and 19–17 before bowing out with a bad arm.

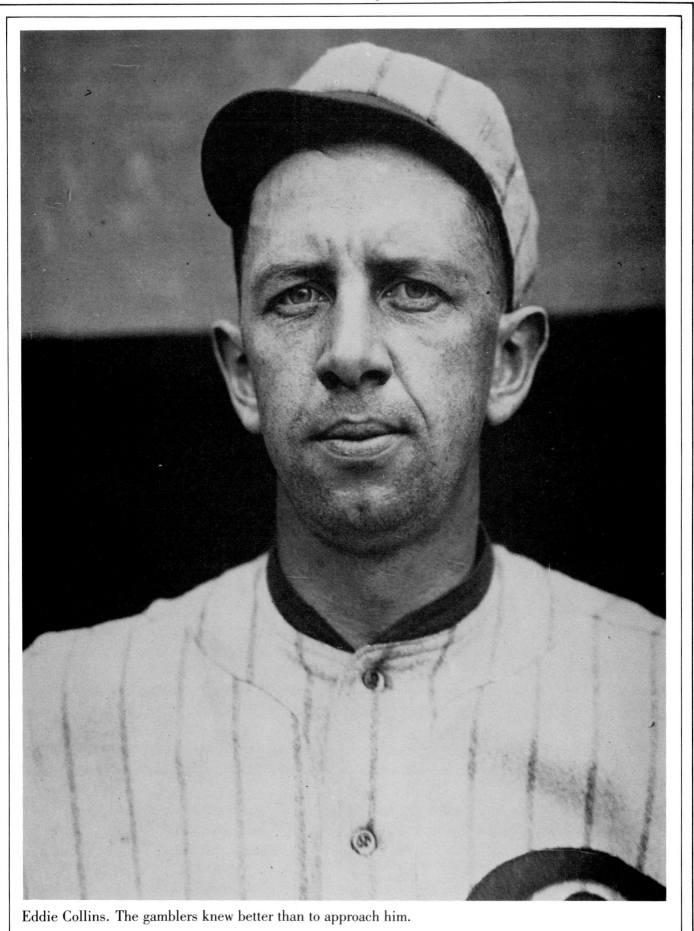

Eddie Collins. The gamblers knew better than to approach him.

Jack Quinn. He was around forever, it seemed, coming up with the Yankees in 1909 and bowing out with Cincinnati in 1933 at the age of forty-nine. In the American League he worked for the Yankees from 1909 through 1912, for the White Sox in 1918, the Yankees again from 1919 through 1921, then the Red Sox and Athletics from 1922 through 1930. Although he never won more than 18 in a season, he kept chucking away and ended with a 212–180 lifetime card.

Ira Flagstead, outfielder with Detroit from 1917 to 1923, when he was traded to the Red Sox. He retired with Pittsburgh in 1930. Ira could hit, going over .300 five times and ringing up a .290 career average.

Carl Mays is remembered primarily for one tragic pitch, which is unfortunate, for the submarine-throwing righty was a big winner. He came up with the Red Sox in 1915 and was a 20-game winner in 1917 and 1918. He was traded to the Yankees in 1919 and was the ace in 1920 and 1921, when he had records of 26–11 and 27–9. Miller Huggins didn't particularly care for him, however, and he was dealt to Cincinnati, where he again won 20 in 1924. Mays pitched until 1929, ending up with an impressive 208–126 career record.

A nattily decked out Ty Cobb on vacation in California in November 1920. As adept with a shotgun as he was with a bat, Ty is showing off some ducks he line-drived.

Ray Chapman. Ray played his entire career for Cleveland, from 1912 to 1920. Three times a .300 hitter, his lifetime average was .278.

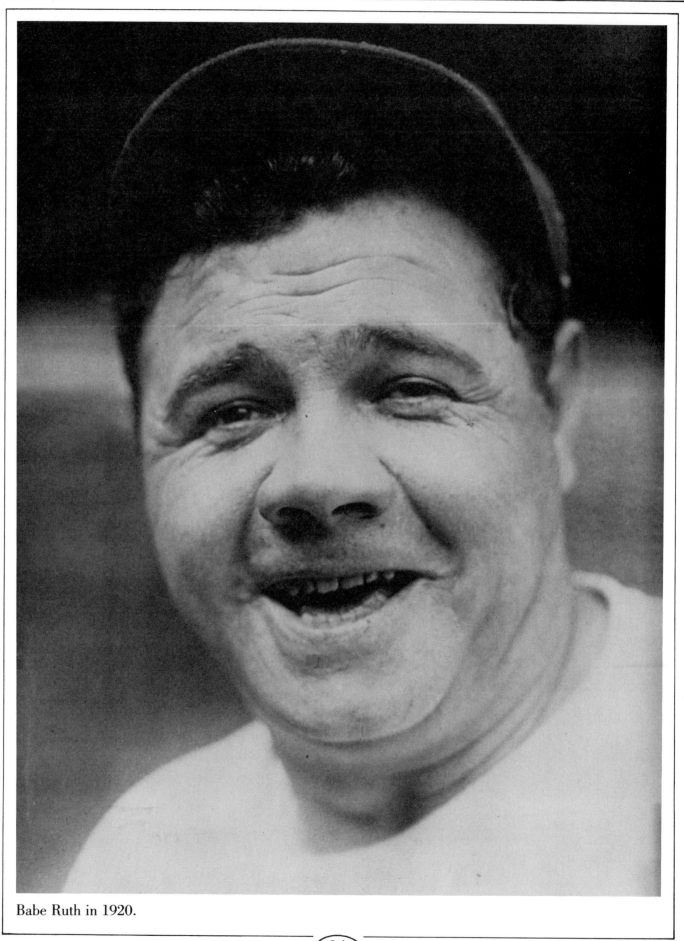

Babe Ruth in 1920.

Hercules in Pinstripes

Little did Boston Red Sox fans realize what a string of flop musicals on Broadway was going to do to their team and, even more, how it was going to affect the history of baseball. The hapless song-and-dancers were produced by a gentleman named Harry Frazee, who also happened to own the Red Sox. In order to keep raising the cash needed to finance his Broadway dreams, Harry began selling off his star players. Conveniently for him, he didn't have to look far to make a deal. His New York office was practically cheek by jowl on Forty-second Street with the offices of the Yankees. By a happy coincidence, the Yankees were owned by Jacob Ruppert, well-heeled scion of a brewery family, who had bucks to spend and a burning desire to win pennants.

The deals between the Red Sox and Yankees began in July 1919 with New York's acquisition of pitcher Carl Mays for two nondescript players and $40,000. In late December 1919 Bostonians were devastated to learn that their pride and joy, Babe Ruth, had been shipped down to New York for around $125,000. It was the most startling deal in baseball history. (Anything to do with Ruth must, it seems, somehow include such words as *most, greatest, biggest*.) And that was only the beginning. Over the next few years there was a steady stream of transactions between the two teams, with the wheat coming to New York and the chaff and the money going to Boston. Following Mays and Ruth from Boston to New York were shortstop Everett Scott, catcher Wally Schang, third baseman Joe Dugan, and pitchers Herb Pennock, Waite Hoyt, Joe Bush, and Sam Jones. The Yankees even grabbed the Red Sox manager, Ed Barrow, installing him as general manager.

By 1923 "The Rape of the Red Sox" was just about complete and the Yankee dynasty, which did not steamroll to a complete halt until 1964, was launched. Appropriately, the Red Sox spent eight of the next nine years in last place, with attendance sinking low enough in some of those years to sprout roots.

Mr. Ruth came to town in 1920 and rewrote the record book. He broke his own home run record with 54—more than any American League *team* had ever hit—batted .376, drove in 137 runs, and compiled a staggering .847 slugging average, still the all-time record. With Ruth driving a recently juiced-up baseball farther than anyone had ever dreamed possible, and doing it with might, majesty, and personality, league attendance took a leap forward to over five million, bettering the previous high by almost a million and a half, and topping the National League's total by more than a million. As a member of a dismal last-place club said a few years later when he went out on the field to take batting practice for a game against the Yankees and, to his amazement, saw a packed house, "It was Ruth. That's what it was. Ruth."

But not even the Babe could do it alone, and in 1920 the Yankees failed to win their first pennant by a mere three games. Cleveland, headed by player-manager Tris Speaker's .388 batting average and right-hander Jim Bagby's 31 wins, slipped in two games ahead of a White Sox team that saw most of its star players suspended in the waning days of the season.

The year 1920 also saw the full blooming of another American League star, one of the purest talents ever to grace a diamond—George Sisler, first baseman of the St. Louis Browns. After batting .353, .341, and .352 the previous three years, Sisler, who like Ruth had begun his career as a left-handed pitcher, tore off a sparkling .407 season, driving out what is still the single-season record for hits, 257. Two years later he did even better, batting .420, leaving Ty Cobb in second

place with a .401 mark.

Yes, Cobb was still poking away, the last of his 12 batting titles now in the books. Ty would keep playing until 1928, batting .323 at the age of forty-one before hanging them up. But it was no longer his game. The game now belonged to Babe Ruth and the men of the big bats, the "full circle" men, the distance hitters. Ty's game of slash and run, of bunt and steal, was rapidly becoming passé. The fans' response to Ruthian baseball was dramatically overwhelming.

With the ball now so live it was almost possible to detect a pulsebeat between the seams, and with pitchers unable to quickly adjust to the new style of play, it became a hitter's game, and the decade of the 1920s became the most glorious hitting circus in baseball history. Most of this thundering took place in the American League. The National had Rogers Hornsby, a slugger to match anyone, but the American had Ruth and Sisler along with the still-lethal Cobb, and Harry Heilmann with his four .390-plus seasons, and then Lou Gehrig and Jimmie Foxx and Al Simmons and Goose Goslin and others.

In 1921 Babe Ruth outdid Babe Ruth with 59 home runs (setting a new home run record for the third year in a row) and 170 runs batted in and an .846 slugging average and a .378 batting average. Along with his 59 homers, Ruth hit 16 triples and 44 doubles and scored 177 runs. It remains, by far, the single-most devastating offensive season by a player in major-league history.

Earned-run averages ballooned as four clubs batted over .300, topped by Detroit's .316—still the all-time American League high. The Tigers were led by Heilmann's league-leading .394, the first of four titles the line-drive-hitting Harry took in odd-numbered years. The sharp-hitting Tiger attack churned out 1,724 hits, also still the all-time league record, but a paucity of quality pitching doomed them to sixth place. In spite of this record-making offense, the Tigers scored 65 fewer runs than the Ruth-led home run-hitting Yankees, who swatted 134 long ones to Detroit's 58.

In 1921, 1922, and 1923 the Yankees won pennants—by a single game over Sisler's Browns in 1922—through a combination of Ruth's bat and all those Red Sox pitchers. Mays won 27 and Hoyt 19 in 1921, Bush 26 and Hoyt 19 in 1922, Jones 21 and Pennock and Bush 19 and Hoyt 17 in 1923.

In 1923 the Yankees opened up a ball park of their own—Yankee Stadium, the biggest, grandest, and most majestic of ball parks, a playground destined to become saturated with baseball history. Appropriately, it was christened on opening day by a game-winning home run by Ruth, who peaked at .393 that year, handsome indeed, but topped by Heilmann's .403. Even when he did nothing at the plate, the Babe was setting records, drawing 170 bases on balls that year (no one else in the league broke a hundred).

An expected fourth straight pennant did not materialize for the Yankees in 1924; instead it went, by a two-game margin, to the Washington Senators, their first ever, leaving the St. Louis Browns as the only pennantless club in the league.

There was a good deal of sentimental appreciation for the Washington pennant, for there he was, still laboring tirelessly, efficiently, uncomplainingly, the great Walter Johnson, now thirty-six years old but still whiplashing his whistlers plateward for a 23–7 record and leading the fraternity in strikeouts, shutouts, and earned-run average (2.72 in a hit-happy season that saw seven of eight clubs bat .281 or better). For once, Walter received some solid support from his teammates, with Goose Goslin batting .344, Sam Rice .334, and Joe Judge .324. The team's spark plug was its twenty-seven-year-old second baseman and manager, Stanley ("Bucky") Harris, a tough-minded individual whom even the great Cobb was careful about sliding into.

Walter delivered a 20–7 season in 1925,

his twelfth and last 20-game year, and again received some solid stickwork from his team as Washington took a second straight pennant, finishing 8½ ahead of a Philadelphia Athletics team that Connie Mack had been patiently and meticulously rebuilding. For only the second time since he joined the Senators in 1907 did Walter find another 20-game winner alongside him (Bob Groom won 24 in 1912). This was spitballing right-hander Stanley Coveleski, who was 20–5. Stanley was no fluke either; he was one of the fine pitchers of his day, the 1925 season being his fifth conquest of 20 wins, the other four coming with Cleveland.

The Yankees dropped to seventh place in 1925, primarily because Ruth missed a third of the season due to an intestinal abscess. The Great Man played in just 98 games, hit 25 home runs, and only teammate Bob Meusel was able to top him with 33. If anyone needed further evidence concerning Mr. Ruth's popularity, here it is: in 1925 he missed about a third of the season; uncoincidentally, Yankee attendance dropped from a little over one million in 1924 to just under 700,000—approximately one third.

Any designs Washington might have had on a third straight pennant in 1926 went asunder with Walter Johnson's thirty-eighty-year-old right arm. The greatest mound dazzler in history finally proved to be human after all, slumping to a 15–16 record in his last full season of work.

Washington finished fourth in 1926, eight games out. Third, six games behind, were the Athletics. Second, just three behind, was Cleveland, thanks largely to a 27–11 year by workhorse right-hander George Uhle, who turned in 32 complete games in 36 starts. Climbing to the top again, prepared for another clutch of three flags in a row, were Miller Huggins' Yankees.

By 1926 the greatest team in baseball history was about to become the Greatest Team in Baseball History. They were all in place now: Ruth, Meusel, and a handsome grey-hound named Earle Combs in the outfield; Dugan at third, rookies Mark Koenig and Tony Lazzeri at short and second, and a shy twenty-three-year-old native New Yorker named Lou Gehrig at first.

Signed out of Columbia University where he was studying to become an engineer, the powerfully built Gehrig had taken over first base from the veteran Wally Pipp the previous June. The story of how Lou finally got off the bench and took over a job that only fatal illness made him relinquish 14 years later has become part of baseball lore. Pipp told Huggins he had a headache and couldn't play. Huggins turned the day's work over to young Gehrig, who went on to play 2,130 consecutive games before sitting down. Pipp was soon traded to Cincinnati, where he no doubt resolved that hereafter he would keep his headaches to himself.

The 1926 Yankees won the pennant by three games; the 1927 club, made up of essentially the same personnel, won by 19, winning a record 110 games and earning the justly deserved title of the Greatest Team ever.

The difference between the 1926 and 1927 squads was that in the latter year a collection of superb players each put together an outstanding individual performance. Ruth, Gehrig, Combs, Meusel, and Lazzeri were seldom better than they were in 1927. The statistics are straight out of fantasyland. Babe unloaded his record 60 home runs, drove in 164, batted .356; Gehrig exploded to stardom with 47 home runs, 175 runs batted in, a .373 batting average; Meusel drove home 103 and batted .337; Combs batted .356 with 231 hits; Lazzeri batted .309 and drove in 102. Up and down the lineup, all year long, they kept hitting and slugging and maiming.

The 1927 Yankees had the top three men in the league in home runs (Ruth, Gehrig, Lazzeri), the top two in slugging average (Ruth, Gehrig), the top three in total bases (Gehrig,

Ruth, Combs), the top two in runs batted in (Gehrig, Ruth), the top two in hits (Combs, Gehrig), the top three in runs scored (Ruth, Gehrig, Combs), the leader in doubles (Gehrig), and the top two in triples (Combs, Gehrig). Collectively, they batted .307

But the hitting was only part of the story. Overlooked, taken for granted, was one of the finest pitching staffs of the era, Herb Pennock (19–8), Waite Hoyt (22–7), Urban Shocker (18–6), Wilcy Moore (19–7), Dutch Ruether (13–6), and George Pipgras (10–3) would have pitched even a team of mere mortals to a pennant. They led in earned-run average and shutouts, were second in complete games, and issued the fewest bases on balls.

The Yankees repeated, as expected, in 1928, but this time it was a struggle. As late as September 8 they were in second place, a whisker behind Connie Mack's rebuilt powerhouse. The next day, the Athletics came into the Stadium for a doubleheader and lost both ends before a crowd reported to be over 85,000. The Yankees stayed on top after that, clinching it two days before the season ended.

It took a remarkable team to make that Yankee squad sweat, and that was exactly what Connie Mack had put together. It included four of baseball's all-time glory names: pitcher Lefty Grove, catcher Mickey Cochrane, first baseman Jimmie Foxx, and outfielder Al Simmons.

Grove, purchased from Baltimore for a little over $100,000, joined the A's in 1925 and quickly replaced the aging Walter Johnson as the league's premier smoke thrower, leading in strikeouts his first seven years. Like Johnson, Lefty was a one-pitch man—a fast ball so fast it looked, according to one opponent, "like a piece of white thread coming to the plate." When asked what Lefty's ball did, how it moved, another contemporary said that it simply got to the plate too fast to have time to move. Unlike the easygoing, good-natured Johnson, Lefty was a dour, humorless man who would throw at hitters when he deemed it necessary, though never at their head. "I would never do that," he said. "I always hit 'em in the pockets." He was not above shaving Ruth now and then, but never Gehrig. "It was best not to wake him up," Lefty said. Apparently a placid Gehrig was wicked enough at the plate; an aroused Gehrig was too much even for Grove to contemplate.

Cochrane, still the choice of many as the all-time catcher, was a match for Grove in competitive fire and temperament. "Lose a one-to-nothing game," said teammate Doc Cramer, "and you didn't want to get into the clubhouse with Grove and Cochrane. You'd be ducking stools and gloves and bats and whatever else would fly." A natural leader, Mickey was also quick enough of foot to occasionally be placed in the leadoff spot by Mack. Cochrane's lifetime .320 average is the highest of any big-league catcher.

Simmons was another testy character. One of the few sticks in the league to match what was coming out of New York in those days, Al four times stroked over .380. Joining the A's in 1924, Simmons averaged .364 for his first eight years and drove in over 100 runs in each of his first 11 years. Cajoled into the batting cage years after his retirement, when he was coaching for the A's, Simmons at bat was still a sight to behold, according to the Yankees' Tommy Henrich. "It was something to see," Henrich recalled. "When Al Simmons would grab hold of a ball bat and dig in, he'd squeeze the handle of that doggone thing and throw the barrel of that bat toward the pitcher in his warm-up swings, and he would look so bloomin' *mad*. In *batting practice*, years after he'd retired! I'd watch him and say to myself, 'Tom, old boy, *that's* the mood you ought to be in when you go to home plate.' "

First baseman Jimmie Foxx, just twenty years old in 1928, was the team's powerhouse. The amiable, always-smiling Foxx was a man of formidable physical strength, capable of hitting a baseball with such authority that he soon became known as "the right-handed Babe Ruth," and there were some who claimed that Jimmie could dispatch a ball even more resoundingly than Ruth. That was a pretty impressive encomium, Ruth being the incomparable in distance hitting as Johnson was the unmatchable olympian in speedball pitching. Fittingly, when Jimmie retired in 1945, his lifetime 534 home runs stood second to Ruth's 714.

Grove, Cochrane, Simmons, and Foxx were aided and abetted by a couple of .300-hitting outfielders named Bing Miller and Mule Haas; second baseman Max Bishop, shortstop Joe Boley, third baseman Jimmy Dykes, and pitchers George Earnshaw and Rube Walberg.

Connie's boys dethroned the Ruth-Gehrig machine in 1929 and did it emphatically— winning 104 games and finishing a handsome 18 lengths in front of the New Yorkers. With the Yankees hitting as lustily as ever, their demise had to be laid at the door of the pitching staff. Hoyt and Pennock suddenly lost it, as did Wilcy Moore. Meanwhile, Mack had Earnshaw winning 24 and Grove 20.

"To be considered great," Connie Mack said, "a team must repeat." His boys carried the injunction forward admirably in 1930, copping another pennant with 102 victories. This was a particularly sock-happy season, the league batting .288 overall. Again pointing up their inadequate pitching, the Yankees as a team batted .309 and finished third. Gehrig was at .379, Ruth .359, Combs .344, and sophomore catcher Bill Dickey .339. Babe and Lou combined to drive in 327 runs, beating out the Foxx-Simmons tandem total of 321. Gehrig was the league leader with 174, followed by Simmons' 165, Foxx's 156, and Ruth's 153.

In a year of inflated earned-run averages, the superman of the mound was Lefty Grove, not only because of his 28–5 record but more so for his 2.54 earned-run average, the next lowest being Cleveland's 25-game winner Wes Ferrell's 3.31. With teams averaging better than five runs per game each that year, Grove's ERA is particularly impressive.

The close of the decade saw Mack and his Athletics kings of the hill, Gehrig swinging into his prime, an aging Ruth still the home run champion, and a scattering through the league of other superb talents, like Washington shortstop Joe Cronin, Cleveland's Ferrell (setting a record by winning 20 or more his first four seasons in the big leagues), and Detroit's flawless second baseman Charlie Gehringer. They were about to lead the league into a decade of even greater dominance, a decade in which the American League was to turn loose upon its diamonds three youngsters destined to become part of the national folklore—Joe DiMaggio, Bob Feller, and Ted Williams.

Tris Speaker, manager and center fielder of the Cleveland Indians. Tris played from 1907 through 1928, mostly for Boston and Cleveland, retiring with a .344 lifetime average.

Sad Sam Jones. Sam pitched in the American League from 1914 through 1935 and made every port of call except Detroit and Philadelphia. His best years were spent with the Red Sox and Yankees. He was 23–16 with Boston in 1921 and 21–8 with the Yankees two years later. Lifetime he was 229–217.

Wheeler ("Doc") Johnston bounced back and forth between the National and American leagues between 1909 and 1922. He was the first baseman on Cleveland's 1920 pennant winners. His career average is .263.

Charlie Jamieson sparkled in the Cleveland outfield from 1919 to 1932. In 1923 he batted .345 with **222** hits, the next year .359 with 213 hits. His career average is .303.

The man whose ready check-book launched the Yankee dynasty—Colonel Jacob Ruppert. (The "Colonel" was an honorary title, conferred upon him by a New York governor.)

Everett Scott, Red Sox shortstop from 1914 to 1921, when he was traded to the Yankees. In 1925 he was dealt to Washington, then to the White Sox a year later, when he retired. Superb in the field, he was a .249 life-time hitter.

S. Coveleski
Clev. A.

Spitballer Stanley Coveleski, American League ace from 1912 to 1928. He was a 20-game winner for Cleveland from 1918 through 1921 and again for Washington in 1925. Overall, Stanley was 214–141.

Larry Gardner, solid third baseman for Boston from 1908 through 1917, the A's for one year, and then Cleveland from 1919 through 1924. Five times a .300 hitter, Larry averaged .289 over his career.

Joe Sewell, the man who replaced Ray Chapman at short for the Indians. Beginning on this note of tragedy, Joe went on to carve out a Hall of Fame career for himself, playing with Cleveland until 1930 and then with the Yankees until 1933. Nine times a .300 hitter, with a high of .353 in 1923, Joe remains the toughest man in baseball history to strike out, fanning just 114 times in 7,132 at bats. Through his last nine seasons he never fanned more than nine times in any single season. Lifetime average: .312.

Jim Bagby surprised a lot of people when he posted a 31–12 record in 1920. Jim, who had joined the Indians in 1916, won 23 in 1917 and then 17 in each of the next two years before chalking up his great year. He could not sustain it, however. He was 14–12 the next year, 4–5 the year after that, and then was soon gone, leaving behind a 127–89 lifetime record.

Cleveland second baseman Bill Wambsganss, the only man to ever make an unassisted triple play in a World Series. He played for Cleveland from 1914 through 1923. He batted .259 lifetime.

Elmer Smith played in the American League from 1914 through 1923. Elmer, an outfielder, had his biggest season with Cleveland in 1920, when he hit .316 and drove in 103 runs; and he had his biggest moment in the World Series that year when he became the first man to hit a grand slam home run in a World Series. He also played for the Senators, Red Sox, and Yankees before finishing up with Cincinnati. Lifetime he batted .267.

Urban ("Red") Faber pitched for the White Sox forever, it seemed. Actually the big right-hander worked from 1914 through 1933, winning over 20 four times with a high of 25 in 1921. When it was all over, Red had a record of 254–212.

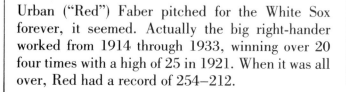

First baseman George Burns rattled around the American League from 1914 through 1929, playing with five different teams, batting over .300 eight times, including seasons of .361 in 1922, .358 in 1926, and .352 in 1918. In 1926 he led the league with 216 hits and 64 doubles. Lifetime average: .307.

The Indians picked up lefty Walter ("Duster") Mails toward the end of the 1920 season to help in the pennant drive. He did just that, winning seven straight games, then added a shutout over Brooklyn in the World Series. Walter could never top himself. He was 14–8 the next year, slumped to 4–7 in 1922 and was gone.

Newly appointed Commissioner Landis in conversation with Tris Speaker in Chicago in 1921. Speaker's uniform indicates the Indians weren't shy about letting people know who did what in 1920.

Howard Ehmke came up with the Tigers in 1916, was traded to the Red Sox in 1923 and to the Athletics in 1926. He won 20 games for the last-place Red Sox in 1923. Overall he was 167–166. Ehmke's most memorable moment came in the opening game of the 1929 World Series, when, as a surprise starter, he beat the Cubs and fanned 13 in setting a series strikeout record. It was the last game he ever won, as he retired the next year.

Mr. Ruth, in person.

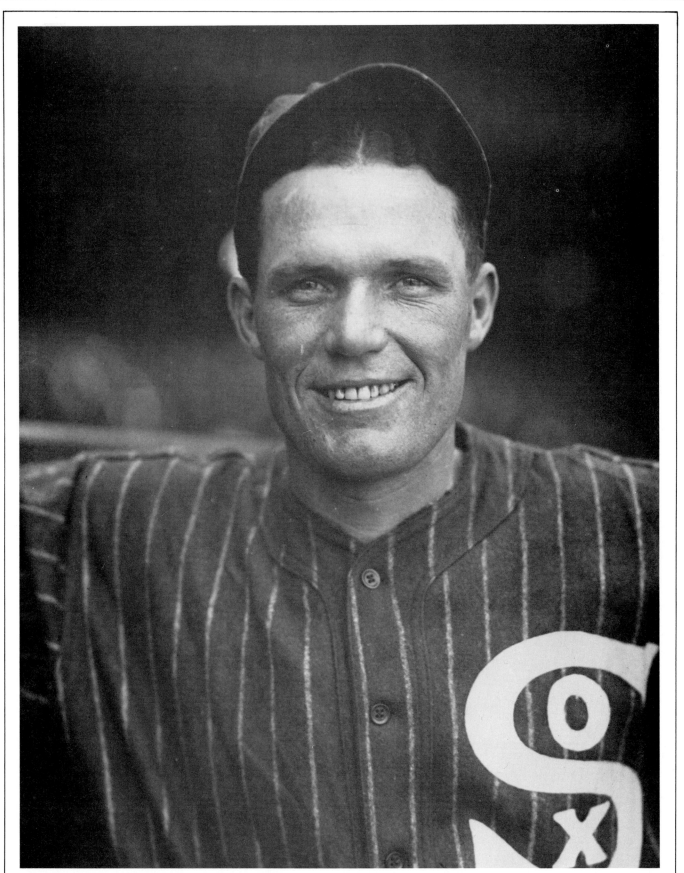

Bibb Falk was a solid performer for the White Sox and Indians from 1920 through 1931, never hitting under .285 and going as high as .352 for the White Sox in 1924. Bibb (that was his real name) was an outfielder. His lifetime average is a fine .314.

Harry Heilmann as a twenty-year-old rookie with Detroit in 1914. Harry was one of the genuine busters of the 1920s. Beginning in 1921 he racked up averages of .394, .356, .403, .346, .393, .367, and .398, taking four batting crowns with those great big numbers. Detroit let him go after the 1929 season and he finished up with Cincinnati in 1932. Lifetime average: .342.

Johnny Bassler, Detroit's regular catcher through the early 1920s. He was a hitting catcher, with averages of .323 in 1922 and .346 in 1924. Lifetime he batted .304.

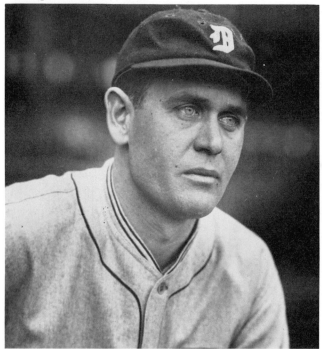

Luzerne ("Lu") Blue, switch-hitting first baseman with Detroit, the St. Louis Browns, and Chicago White Sox from 1921 through 1932. Lu went over .300 five times and ended with a .287 mark.

Old-timers claimed there were few better defensive center fielders than Chicago's Johnny Mostil, who hawked them out of Chicago skies from 1918 through 1929. Along with his reputation as a glove, Johnny left behind a .301 career average.

Except for one April afternoon in 1922 it was a journeyman's career for Charlie Robertson. Charlie pitched for the White Sox from 1922 to 1925, then briefly for the Browns before two undistinguished seasons with the Boston Braves. His lifetime record was 49–80, his best year 1922, when he was 14–15. But on April 30, 1922, the rookie right-hander spun one of baseball's rarities—a perfect game, setting down flawlessly a Detroit lineup that included Cobb, Veach, and Heilmann.

From 1920 through 1922 George Sisler had batting averages of .407, .371, and .420, and there were some who felt he still had not reached his peak. Eye trouble, however, kept him out of action the entire 1923 season, and when he came back he was never the same again. He played from 1915 through 1930, most of the time with the Browns. Lifetime average: .340.

William ("Baby Doll") Jacobson, another heavy clouter in the Browns' outfield in the early 1920s. Baby Doll joined the club in 1915 and got going in 1919 with the first of seven straight .300-plus seasons, including .355 and .352 efforts in 1920–1921. He retired in 1927, playing his last season with the Red Sox, Indians, and Athletics. His career average is .311.

Wally Gerber, St. Louis Browns shortstop through most of the 1920s. He finished up with the Red Sox in 1929 with a .257 career average.

Jack Tobin, sharp-hitting Browns outfielder from 1916 through 1925. Jack hit over .300 seven times, with a high of .352 in 1921, a year in which he collected 236 hits, one of four consecutive 200-hit seasons for him. He wound up with the Red Sox in 1927, batting .310, one point over his lifetime mark.

Right-hander Eddie Rommel pitched for the Athletics from 1920 through 1932. His best year was 1922, when he was 27–13. Overall he was 171–119.

Ken Williams, third member of the Browns' belting outfield in the early 1920s. Ken was with the Browns from 1918 through 1927, then going to Boston for the final two years of his career. He hit over .300 ten times, with .357 in 1923 his high-water mark. He led with 39 home runs and 155 runs batted in, in 1922. Lifetime average: .319.

Hank Severeid caught for the Browns from 1915 through 1924. A good-hitting catcher, he had a career mark of .289.

George Uhle, strong right-hander for Cleveland and Detroit from 1919 to 1933. George was at his best in 1923, with a 26–16 record, and 1926, when he was 27–11. He won 200 on the nose and lost 166.

In this bit of action in June 1922, Bing Miller of the Athletics is out trying to steal home. The Yankees' Wally Schang is applying the tag.

George ("Sarge") Connally pitched for the White Sox and Indians from 1921 to 1934. Sarge was one of the first relief specialists. His lifetime record was 49–60.

Griffith Stadium, home of the Washington Senators from 1911 until they departed for Minnesota in 1960.

Bucky Harris. He played second base for Washington from 1919 through 1928, batting .274 lifetime. He was a big-league manager for 29 years.

Ossie Bluege, one of the finest fielding third basemen in American League history. Ossie spent all 18 of his big-league seasons with Washington, from 1922 to 1939, compiling a .272 batting average.

Roger Peckinpaugh came up with Cleveland in 1910 and was traded to the Yankees in 1913, where he was a first-class shortstop until 1922, when he was dealt to Washington. He finished up with the White Sox in 1927. He batted .259 lifetime.

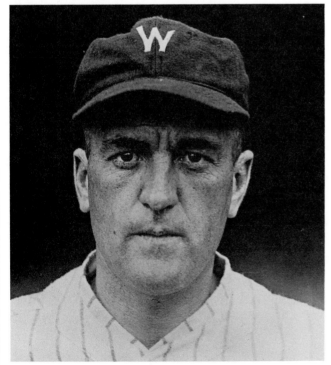

Joe Judge, first baseman on Washington's pennant winners in 1924 and 1925. Joe played first for the Senators from 1915 through 1932, hitting over .300 nine times and winding up with a career mark of .297.

Sam Rice, one of the steadiest of all hitters. He joined the Senators in 1915 and played until 1934. An outfielder, Sam batted over .300 13 times and never, in 20 years, batted under .293. He collected 2,987 hits in his career (those last 13 never seemed to interest him) and batted .322.

Herold ("Muddy") Ruel, American League catcher from 1915 to 1934. Muddy caught for everybody except the Athletics and Indians. His longest stint with one club was with Washington, from 1923 through 1930. He batted .275 through it all.

George Mogridge, a talented left-hander who worked American League mounds with four different teams from 1911 through 1925. George twice was an 18-game winner with Washington, in 1921 and 1922. Lifetime he was 134–129.

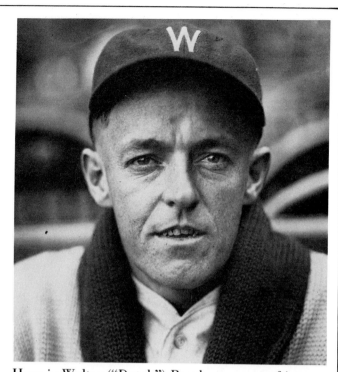

Here is Walter ("Dutch") Ruether, a man of impeccable timing. After a successful National League career, he joined the Senators in 1925, in time to help pitch them to a pennant, with an 18–7 record. Midway through the next season he was traded to the Yankees, where he cashed series checks in 1926 and 1927. Then he retired. Overall the left-hander was 137–95.

Outfielder Bill Lamar had bounced around with little distinction with the Yankees, Red Sox, and Dodgers when he joined the Athletics in 1924. Bill gave Connie Mack two years of .330 and .356 efficiency, then began to fade. By 1928 he was gone.

Fred ("Firpo") Marberry, Washington relief ace from 1923 through 1932. He also pitched on two Detroit pennant winners in 1934 and 1935. Lifetime he was 147–89.

Leon ("Goose") Goslin, outfielder, slugger, and RBI man par excellence. The Goose arrived in 1921 with Washington and put in some time with St. Louis and Detroit and Washington again. Wherever he was, he hit. He went over .300 11 times, leading the league in 1928 with .379. He also knocked in 100 or more runs 11 times. He retired in 1938 with a .316 average. (It is not known if Goose ever used that barber-pole bat he is holding in a game.)

Two of the American League's patriarchal figures, Connie Mack (left) and Clark Griffith giving each other five.

Absalom ("Al") Wingo, outfielder with Detroit from 1924 through 1928. In 1925 Al sizzled to a .370 season, but that was completely out of character. He retired with a .308 lifetime.

Bob ("Fats") Fothergill, another big bat in the Detroit lineup from 1922 to 1930. He later played with the White Sox and Red Sox, retiring in 1933 with a .326 lifetime average.

"If he had pitched for the Yankees he would have won four hundred games." That's what Joe McCarthy said abut Ted Lyons. But Ted didn't pitch for the Yankees, he pitched for the White Sox, from 1923 to 1946, winning over 20 three times. Career record: 260–230.

Wally Pipp, Lou Gehrig's immediate predecessor as Yankee first baseman. Wally covered the sack for the Yanks from 1915 until muscled aside by Lou in 1925. Wally was the American League home run champ with 12 in 1916 and 9 in 1917. His lifetime average is .281.

Outfielder Henry ("Heinie") Manush had a 17-year big-league career, from 1923 through 1939, most of it spent with the Tigers, Browns, and Senators. A consummate line-drive hitter, Heinie led the league with a .378 average in 1926. Two years later he hit .378 again, with 241 hits. He batted over .300 11 times, 8 times over .330, which is his lifetime average.

Three White Sox stalwarts in 1926. Left to right: Bibb Falk, first baseman Earl Sheely, third baseman Willie Kamm. Earl was a lifetime .300 hitter, Willie batted .281.

Yankee Manager Miller Huggins. Hug won six pennants for the Yankees in the 1920s. He died suddenly at the end of the 1929 season.

Babe Ruth.

Lou Gehrig in 1926.

The infield of the 1927 Yankees. Left to right: Lou Gehrig, Tony Lazzeri, Mark Koenig, Joe Dugan. Lazzeri played for the Yankees from 1926 to 1937, driving in over 100 runs seven times; Koenig was with New York from 1925 to 1930, when he was dealt to Detroit; Dugan came to New York in 1922 via Philadelphia and Boston, playing for the Yanks until 1928.

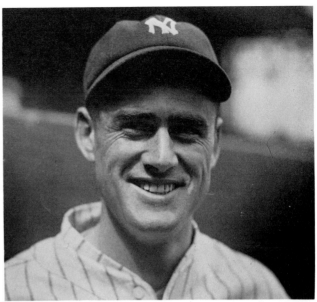

Earle Combs, Yankee center fielder from 1924 through 1935. Earle's best year was 1927, when he batted .356 with 231 hits. Overall he batted .325.

Bob Meusel, left-fielder on six Yankee pennant winners in the 1920s. Bob hit for average (.309 lifetime) and with power; he also had what many regarded as the league's strongest throwing arm. With the Yankees from 1920 through 1929, Bob batted over .300 seven times and in 1925 led with 33 home runs and 138 runs batted in.

Right-hander Waite Hoyt pitched in the big leagues from 1918 through 1938. The Yankees obtained him from the Red Sox in 1921 and Waite had his top years in New York. In 1927 he was 22–7, in 1928 23–7. Lifetime he was 237–182.

Herb Pennock.

Right-hander Wilcy Moore was a thirty-year-old rookie for the Yankees in 1927 and he gave them a memorable year. Working out of the bullpen most of the time, he ran up a 19–7 record. He pitched until 1933 but never came close to weaving that magic again, retiring with a 51–44 record.

Urban Shocker, spitballing righty who pitched for the Yankees, Browns, and Yankees again from 1916 through 1928. He won 20 or better four straight seasons for the Browns, with a high of 27 in 1921. He won 19 for the 1926 Yankees, 18 the next year. Lifetime record: 188–117.

Ty Cobb in 1927. Cobb played his final two years for Connie Mack. In 1927 the forty-year-old Cobb batted .357; in 1928, .323.

Oscar Melillo, St. Louis Browns second baseman from 1926 to 1935. Oscar finished up with the Red Sox in 1937. For his dozen years he batted .260.

After five years in the National League, Lew Fonseca joined the Indians in 1927. In 1929 Lew won the batting crown with a .369 average. It was the first baseman's last full season. He retired with the White Sox in 1933, leaving behind a .316 lifetime average.

Tony Lazzeri. Tony's best year was 1929, when he batted .354. He batted .300 five times, .292 for his career.

Lefty Grove.

George Pipgras pitched for the Yankees in the 1920s and early 1930s before being traded to the Red Sox. His big year was 1928, when he was 24–13. Lifetime he was 102–73.

Mickey Cochrane's lifetime average of .320 is the highest of any catcher in history. A beaning by the Yankees' Bump Hadley in 1937 ended Mickey's career and almost cost him his life.

Jimmie Foxx. Jimmie played for the A's and Red Sox from 1925 until 1942, when he drifted into the National League. He had 13 consecutive years of 100 or more runs batted in. He hit 58 home runs in 1932, 50 in 1938. Lifetime batting average: .325.

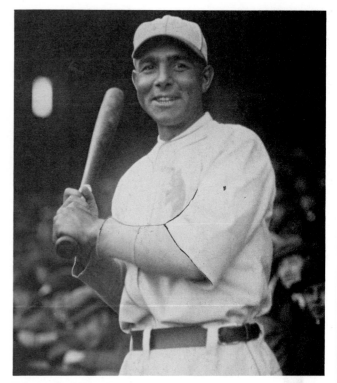

Al Simmons. One of the wickedest of all hitters, Al played from 1924 to 1944, having his heyday years with the A's from 1924 to 1932. He drove in over 100 runs his first 11 years in the majors, won two batting crowns, with .381 in 1930 and .390 the next year. He also batted .384 in 1925 and .392 in 1927, losing out to Harry Heilmann each year. He had 253 hits in 1925. Lifetime average: .334.

Edmund ("Bing") Miller, one of the sharp stickers in Connie Mack's outfield in the 1920s. Playing from 1921 through 1936, Bing topped .300 nine times. His career mark is .312.

Shibe Park, Philadelphia, in 1929.

George ("Mule") Haas, another one of Connie Mack's outfield steadies in the 1929–1931 championship years. Mule played for the A's from 1928 through 1932, then was traded to the White Sox. He retired in 1938 with a batting average of .292.

Third baseman Sammy Hale played for the Athletics from 1923 through 1929, hitting .345 in 1925. His career average is .302.

George Earnshaw, whom some people said threw as hard as Grove. George pitched for the A's from 1928 to 1933 before being traded to the White Sox. He won over 20 games in each of the Athletics' pennant years. He retired in 1936 with a 127–93 lifetime record.

Max Bishop. Max was Connie Mack's second baseman from 1924 through 1933. He played two more years with the Red Sox and then retired. His top average was .316 in 1928. Lifetime he was .271.

Joe Boley was at shortstop for the A's from 1927 to 1932. Joe batted .311 in his rookie year, well above his career average of .269.

Jimmy Dykes, a vivid character on the scene as player and manager for more than half a century. He played for the A's from 1918 to 1932, then for the White Sox until 1939. Playing most of his games at third base, Jimmy stroked away steadily to a .280 career average. When Connie Mack finally retired as manager of the A's in 1951 it was Dykes who replaced him. He also managed the White Sox for 13 years and put in managerial stints with Baltimore, Cincinnati, Detroit, and Cleveland.

Left-hander George ("Rube") Walberg, the third man of Connie Mack's fine trio of starters in 1929–1931. Rube pitched for Connie from 1924 through 1933, then put in four more years with the Red Sox. He won 20 in 1931 and overall was 155–141.

Wes Ferrell set a record by winning over 20 games in each of his first four big-league seasons with Cleveland, beginning in 1929. He later added two more 20-game seasons with the Red Sox. Tough, temperamental, and handsome, Wes worked the big-league mounds from 1929 to 1941, ending up with a 193–128 lifetime record.

Lou Gehrig and Hank Greenberg.

4
Heroes and More Heroes

In 1931 Robert Moses ("Lefty") Grove put on the most scintillating season-long display of quality pitching in decades. In fact, not since Smokey Joe Wood was 34–5 in 1912 and Walter Johnson 36–7 a year later had a pitcher been so splendidly unbeatable. Grove put together an altogether unreasonable 31–4 record. And again, it was not just his teammates' punishing stickwork that elevated Lefty to such breathtaking heights. The swiftie was in a class by himself with a 2.05 earned-run average (the next lowest was New York's own Lefty—Gomez—with 2.63; no one else in the league checked in under 3.00) and leads in strikeouts, shutouts, and complete games.

The highlight of Grove's season was a 16-game winning streak, tying him for the league record with Smokey Joe Wood and Walter Johnson. The streak was broken by a 1–0 loss to the St. Louis Browns, on a misplayed fly ball no less, after which Lefty redecorated the Athletic clubhouse with the subtlety of a runaway tractor.

Grove's chief conspirator in driving the Athletics to a third straight pennant was Al Simmons, who took a meat-ax to American League pitchers that year with a .390 average. The A's put together winning streaks of 17 in May and 13 in July as they won 107 and came in 13½ ahead of a Yankee powerhouse still a bit short of first-rate pitching. Ruth and Gehrig tied for the lead with 46 home runs apiece and Gehrig set the all-time American League runs batted in record with 184.

A year later, however, the Yankees, who had seen the Athletics end their three-year reign in 1929, now returned the favor. Getting the pitching they had been lacking, from Lefty Gomez (24–7), Red Ruffing (18–7), and rookie

Johnny Allen (17–4), the New Yorkers gave Joe McCarthy his first pennant in New York in his second season in charge.

Ruth, now a rotund thirty-seven, still had enough left to club 41 home runs and bat .341, while Gehrig continued his lusty belting. The league's biggest home run thunder that year, however, came booming out of Philadelphia, where Jimmie Foxx put together a season of unremitting cannon fire, connecting for 58 home runs, a .364 batting average, and driving in 169. Lefty Grove, after a three-year run during which he put up a 79–14 won-lost record, "slipped" to 25–10, with a 2.84 ERA, the only ERA under 3.00 in the league that year.

In 1933 the Washington Senators surprised everyone by slipping past the two titans who had been dominating the league the past half-dozen years and finishing seven ahead of the Yankees and 19½ in front of the Athletics. As it had been in 1924–1925, the club was spearheaded by a tough young playing manager in the middle of the infield. Before it had been Bucky Harris, now it was Joe Cronin, a handsome, lantern-jawed San Francisco Irishman who took over the team that season and showed the boys how to do it, with a .309 batting average and 118 runs batted in. The twenty-six-year-old Cronin, who had a flair for leadership (he eventually became American League president), had some solid whackers around him, even if they didn't hit many home runs. Heinie Manush, Goose Goslin, and Fred Schulte were the outfield, and they popped singles and doubles all year, while Joe Kuhel at first base, Buddy Myer at second, Cronin, and defensive whiz Ossie Bluege gave Washington the best infield it ever had. Luke Sewell was behind the plate, receiving the artistry of 24-game winner Alvin Crowder and 22-game winner Earl Whitehill.

Washington's victory continued a 12-year string of pennant winners in the eastern division; the last victory cry from the West had been Cleveland's in 1920. But things were about to change, at least temporarily. It was, in fact, the last flag the Senators would ever win. And the Philadelphia Athletics and Connie Mack had already won their last pennant.

Despite the powerful club Mack still had (Foxx took the Triple Crown in 1933 and Grove rolled to a 24–8 season), attendance in Philadelphia was dropping like a January thermometer. The decline began after the 1929 season, when Connie counted over 830,000 noses; by 1933 less than 300,000 paying customers showed up. There were several reasons for this, one being, of course, the Depression, which had cut overall league attendance by a million and a half since 1929. Connie had also taken a personal bath in the stock market and, in addition, found himself with a star-studded team with a heavy payroll.

So for the second time in his career, Mack began the breakup of a great team. In a few years time he had divested himself of his star players, selling them off for ready cash. Simmons, Haas, Dykes, and Earnshaw went to Chicago; Foxx, Grove, and Bishop soon were getting their mail in Boston (where an energetic young millionaire named Tom Yawkey had recently taken over and was trying to exorcise the ghost of Harry Frazee by buying star players); and Cochrane went to Detroit where he became catcher and manager.

In 1934 the Tigers promptly cashed dividends on their $100,000 outlay for Cochrane. The fiery catcher, installed as manager, was just what the Tigers needed. Taking a cast that included the impeccable Charlie Gehringer at second, a youngster at first base with a thunderous bat named Hank Greenberg, Billy Rogell at short, Marv Owen at third, and good-hitting outfielders Goose Goslin, Pete Fox, Jo-Jo White, and Gerald ("Gee") Walker, Mickey whiplashed them to Detroit's first pennant since the Ty Cobb days of 1909. On the mound the Tigers had right-handers Lynwood ("Schoolboy") Rowe, whose 24 wins included a midsummer 16-game winning streak that tied him for the record with

Johnson, Wood, and Grove; and 22-game winner Tommy Bridges, whom everybody said broke off the league's best curve ball.

This Tiger array, batting .300 as a unit, outran the Yankees by seven games, obliterating a Triple Crown effort by Gehrig and Gomez's masterful 26–5 season. If they had been handing out Cy Young Awards in those days, Lefty would have been the unanimous choice, leading in wins, winning percentage, complete games, innings pitched, strikeouts, shutouts, and earned-run average, as well as quips (he attributed his success to "clean living and a fast outfield").

It was in that Depression year of 1934 that baseball fans were given sad and sobering evidence that even Babe Ruth was mortal. At thirty-nine years of age, the mightiest slugger of them all was large of belly and slow of foot. In the gray light of his career, the Babe turned in a season that lesser men would have dined out on all winter: 22 home runs, 84 runs batted in, a .288 batting average. But for Babe Ruth, those numbers spelled the end. The Yankees let him go after the season and he joined the Boston Braves in the National League, but the magic was irretrievably gone, and early in June 1935, he retired.

Detroit kept it going for another year, supporting a strong pitching staff of Rowe (19–13), Bridges (21–10), Eldon Auker (18–7), and Alvin Crowder (16–10) with a solid attack. Hank Greenberg tied Jimmie Foxx for the lead with 36 home runs and ran away and hid with the RBI title with 170—Gehrig was second with 119. Gehringer, that model of quiet, deadly efficiency, batted .330, drove in 108 runs, fanned just 16 times in 610 at bats, and fielded as if he had invented second base. Pete Fox and skipper Cochrane added .300 bats to a potent attack that batted .290 as a team. For Cochrane, it was his fifth pennant winner in seven years.

Boston owner Tom Yawkey, dead serious about bringing a pennant to town, had shelled out a whopping 250,000 Depression-year dollars for Washington's shortstop-manager Joe Cronin, installing Joe in those slots for the Red Sox. Symptomatic of the frustration Yawkey was destined to experience through most of the many, free-spending years he owned the club, the Sox finished fourth despite Cronin and despite 45 wins from Wes Ferrell and Lefty Grove.

The Ruth-less Yankees finished just three games behind Detroit in 1935. For the rest of the league, that was ominous. Studying the strong Yankee lineup in 1935 one notes a solid infield in Lou Gehrig, Tony Lazzeri, Frank Crosetti, and Red Rolfe; perhaps the greatest of all catchers in Bill Dickey; and two fine outfielders in George Selkirk and Ben Chapman. They needed one more good man in the outfield. And he was on the way.

In 1933 the most sought-after minor-league player in the country was San Francisco's nineteen-year-old center fielder Joe DiMaggio. The youngster was the sensation of the Pacific Coast League, batting .340, driving in 169 runs, and covering the outfield with antelope grace. He also enlivened the California summer with a 61-game hitting streak. The San Francisco club was deluged with offers for Joe's contract. The club decided to hold on to their young star for another year, reasoning that he could only improve and thus increase his value. Midway through the 1934 season, however, DiMaggio suffered a knee injury while doing nothing more strenuous than getting out of a cab. Shelved for much of the season, he became suspect in the eyes of big-league clubs.

The Yankees, however, decided to take a gamble. For $25,000 and a clutch of minor leaguers, they acquired DiMaggio's contract, agreeing to San Francisco's stipulation that Joe play another year in the Pacific Coast League. The Yankee gamble looked pretty good after that 1935 season. DiMaggio played in 172 games (Pacific Coast League schedules were longer), collected 270 hits, and batted .398.

Babe Ruth had built the Yankee image into a personification of awesome power; Joe DiMaggio changed it to one of cool, businesslike efficiency. Off the field he was an enigma—aloof, shy, snobbish, insecure, no one was quite sure which; maybe a bit of each. On the field he was dynamic and charismatic. He was class and style and grace; probably the most complete ballplayer who ever lived. Despite a total absence of what might be called "the common touch" (which Ruth possessed to exorbitant degrees), DiMaggio's chemistry somehow blended perfectly into the dreams of the bleacher fan—exciting worshipful adulation. He became, after Ruth, the most idolized of ballplayers, projecting a magnetism and a mystique that decades after his retirement was still capable of enthralling packed stadiums on Old-Timers Days.

With DiMaggio in the lineup in 1936, the Yankee dynasty, the most formidable in all sports history, was truly launched. Joe McCarthy's team made a shambles of the league in taking four consecutive pennants, by margins of 19½, 13, 9½, and 17 games. Averaging nearly seven runs a game, the 1936 club had five men drive in over 100 runs, six men bat over .300

The hitting in the American League in 1936 was murderous from top to bottom, with 18 men driving in over 100 runs (only five could do as well in the National League). Cleveland's muscular first baseman Hal Trosky was the RBI leader with 162, while Chicago's Luke Appling led the league with a .388 batting average, highest ever for a shortstop. Gehrig, rolling along day in and day out, never missing a game, pounded 49 home runs to top the league.

Oddly enough, despite all of this hitting (five teams in the league hit over .290), the most electrifying performer in the American League in 1936 was a seventeen-year-old right-hander who actually did not start his first big-league game until the end of August. His name was Bob Feller, he was the second of 1936's two golden rookies, and there was something so quintessentially American about him that he leaped instantly, firmly, and permanently into the pantheon of national sports heroes. He was mid-America, out of the Iowa corn belt, with a plowboy's walk and strength. Tutored by a baseball-loving father on a makeshift diamond carved out of the family farm, he became the only genuine prodigy in baseball history. He was rough-hewn and unsophisticated, but immediately unawed and confident on the mound, with the confidence that all fast ballers bring to the hill with them. And fast he was. Was he as quick as Walter Johnson? "The difference," one old-timer said, "was so slight as to make no difference."

Cleveland scout Cy Slapnicka, badgered for months by bug-eyed Iowans, finally stopped off in the town of Van Meter (both Slapnicka and Van Meter, Iowa, have been imperishably footnoted by baseball historians) on a trip west to have a look at the youngster. The skepticism in Slapnicka's mind melted under the heat of Feller's first swifty. The scout signed the boy right then and there and reported back to his employers that he had just signed "the greatest pitcher he had ever seen." As a bonus, Feller received an autographed baseball and a one-dollar bill. As a bargain, the transaction goes into the books with the acquisition of Manhattan Island and the purchase of Alaska.

Staying with the Indians as a nonroster player through most of 1936, Bob Feller was finally activated after the All-Star Game and given a start on August 23 against the Browns. He made headlines by fanning 15. A few weeks later, he tied a league record by striking out 17 Philadelphia Athletics. "That hit the newspapers like thunder and lightning," Feller said, "and I guess that's when people began to realize I was for real."

In 1938 Detroit's Hank Greenberg put on one of baseball's most dramatic season-long power displays. With five games left to play, the Tiger slugger had 58 home runs, two short of Ruth's 1927 record. He went the next three games without hitting any long ones, then came down to the final game of the season facing the Indians in a doubleheader. In the opener, Greenberg had the misfortune of running into Bob Feller. The Cleveland buzz-baller, now all of nineteen years old, not only stopped Hank from losing any baseballs but also fanned a record 18 batters (ironically, Feller lost the game, 4–1). The best Big Henry could manage in the second game was three singles, thus falling two homers short of Ruth. Greenberg's tremendous year overshadowed a fine showing by Boston's Jimmie Foxx, who hit 50 home runs of his own.

Eight games into the 1939 season, a season in which the Yankees became the first American League team to take four consecutive pennants, one of the game's majestic records and careers came to a sudden, and tragic, halt.

It had been a painful and frustrating spring training for Lou Gehrig. The Yankee great could not seem to get untracked. His bat was slow, his fielding unsteady, his overall performance sluggish. His teammates kidded him, telling him he was getting old—he was nearly thirty-six. But clearly, there was something wrong.

When the season began, Gehrig had a consecutive game string of 2,122, long ago having broken Everett Scott's record of 1,307. (Scott, Gehrig's teammate on the Yankees, had ended his streak in the same 1925 season that Lou began his.) So, eight games into the season, with his streak now standing at 2,130 games, Lou Gehrig, hitting .143 with no extra base hits and but one run batted in, went to Joe McCarthy and asked to be taken out of the lineup. McCarthy had been waiting for this, unwilling to embarrass his great first baseman by benching him. The date was May 2, 1939, in Detroit.

Two months later Gehrig, slowing down perceptibly almost daily, went to the Mayo Clinic in Rochester, Minnesota. There he learned he was suffering from a neuromuscular disease, amyotrophic lateral sclerosis. There was no known cure for the rare disease. On July 4, between games of a doubleheader on Lou Gehrig Appreciation Day at Yankee Stadium, a huge throng listened to Gehrig say, in a speech simple and modest in its eloquence, that he considered himself "the luckiest man on the face of the earth." Two years later, the most durable of ballplayers was dead.

Ruth had been the King, Gehrig the Crown Prince, the two most formidable left-handed sluggers of all time. But already in the league when Gehrig retired was a rail-thin left-handed thumper with the most flawless whiplash swing seen since the days of Joe Jackson. His name was Ted Williams and he was with the Red Sox.

His ambition as a youngster was to become the greatest hitter who ever lived. In the opinion of many a qualified observer, that is exactly what he became. Just twenty years old when he joined the Sox in 1939, the San Diego-born Williams was discovered by Eddie Collins, then general manager for the Red Sox. Collins was on the West Coast to scout San Diego's dazzling second baseman Bobby Doerr. Eddie's mind was on Doerr when he saw Williams step into the batting cage to unlimber. History is vague on whether it took one, two, or three swings for Collins' eyes to pop. The old Athletic second baseman returned home from "history's greatest scouting trip" with deals for Williams and Doerr in his hip pocket.

Williams had everything, beginning with high ambition and deep resolve. He had the eyesight, the judgment, the coordination, the power, the discipline at bat. He would not swing at a pitch a quarter of an inch off the plate. His judgment of a pitched ball became so legendary that some umpires almost automatically called a ball any close pitch that Ted Williams did not offer at.

It did not take long before everything on the field stopped when Williams stepped into the cage to take his rips. Only Ruth and Hornsby before him evoked such awe and respect. He soon became the most charismatic hitter since Ruth; his mere appearance in the on-deck circle was enough to send currents of anticipation through a crowd.

In his rookie year, the intense youngster with the beach-boy good looks batted .327, hit 31 home runs, and led with 145 runs batted in. In the lineup with Williams was Jimmie Foxx with a .360 average, Doerr batting .318, player-manager Cronin .308, outfielder Doc Cramer .311. On the mound the thirty-nine-year-old Lefty Grove, pitching with guile and craft now, his fast one long since cooled, was 15–4 with a record ninth earned-run-average title. Red Sox fans, however, had to content themselves with the glories of these individual performances as their club finished second, 17 games behind the Yankees.

The New Yorkers were beginning to enjoy the fruits of a shrewdly put together and carefully nurtured farm system that had been built by General Manager Ed Barrow and Farm Director George Weiss. Homegrown talents included second baseman Joe Gordon, outfielder Charlie Keller, and pitchers Spud Chandler and Atley Donald, among others. For Joe DiMaggio, 1939 was a banner year. After flirting with .400 for much of the season, the Yankee Clipper ended with a .381 batting average, taking his first batting title.

A fifth consecutive Yankee pennant in 1940 seemed inevitable. But the club the Yankees had dethroned as champions in 1936, the Tigers, came on to take an exciting three-team race, finishing one game ahead of Cleveland and two ahead of New York. Cleveland stayed till the end thanks to Bob Feller's 27 wins (including baseball's only opening day no-hitter) and a fine season from young shortstop Lou Boudreau. The Yankees suffered an up-and-down-the-lineup hitting drop, their .259 team average 28 points under the previous year's. DiMaggio, with a league-leading .352 average, was the only regular to clear the .300 mark.

For the Tigers, big Henry Greenberg led the way with a .340 average and league-leading figures in home runs (41) and runs batted in (150). Sophomore outfielder Barney McCosky also batted .340, the ageless Gehringer .313, and first baseman Rudy York .316 with 33 homers and 134 runs batted in. The Tigers found an ace in colorful, much-traveled right-hander Louis Norman ("Bobo") Newsom. Bobo moved from team to team 16 times in his long career; he pitched for Washington on five separate occasions, always re-acquired, it was said, because Clark Griffith enjoyed Bobo's pinochle game. A likable, irrepressible sort, Newsom got his nickname from his habit of calling everyone else "Bobo." Picked up by the Athletics in a trade, he walked into the clubhouse and greeted Connie Mack, baseball's nearest approximation of sainthood, with, "Hi, Bobo." Later, Newsom was taken aside by some of the team's elder statesmen and cautioned, "Around here we call him 'Mr. Mack.'" In 1940 Bobo, once described by a teammate as having "a rubber arm and head to match," put together his finest year, pitching Detroit to a pennant with a 21–5 record.

At the end of the decade, the American League stood at what was probably the pinnacle of its supremacy, outdrawing the National League by more than a million paid admissions. Offensively, there was no comparison between the two major leagues. In 1940 the American outhomered its rival, 883 to 688; outscored them, 6,147 to 5,421; outbatted them, .271 to .264. The game's most prodigious overachievers were employed by what sports writers called "the junior circuit." The American League had Joe DiMaggio, Bill Dickey, Ted Williams, Jimmie Foxx, Hank Greenberg, Bob Feller. The tide would be turning, however, after a world war and a postwar revolution named Jackie Robinson.

Babe Ruth surrounded by some of his favorite people. The place is Los Angeles, the year, 1931.

Ben Chapman, talented, sometimes outspoken out-fielder with the Yankees from 1930 to 1936. Ben learned to keep his suitcase packed, going on to play with Washington, Boston, Cleveland, and Chicago in the American League, and then Brooklyn and Philadelphia in the National, retiring in 1946. Be-tween all the packing and unpacking he batted .302.

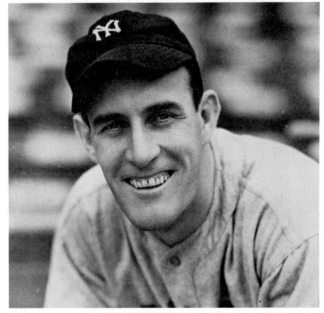

His contemporaries remember right-hander Johnny Allen as one of the toughest and meanest of pitchers. He was also a winner, ringing up a 17–4 rookie sea-son with the Yankees in 1934 and 20–10 and 15–1 seasons with Cleveland in 1936 and 1937. When he hung them up in 1944 Johnny had a 142–75 record for a .654 winning percentage. The only American League pitchers to do better are Whitey Ford, Lefty Grove, and Vic Raschi.

Three future Hall of Famers in 1931. Left to right: Bill Dickey, Lefty Gomez, and Lou Gehrig of the New York Yankees. Dickey, considered by many the greatest of all catchers, played for the Yankees from 1928 to 1946, batting .313, with a high of .362 in 1936. Gomez was a four-time 20-game winner, with a lifetime record of 189–102.

Detroit's incomparable second baseman, Charlie Gehringer. He covered the sack for the Tigers from 1924 to 1942, hitting over .300 thirteen times with his high a league-leading .371 in 1937. He had seven 200-hit seasons. He led second basemen in fielding eight times. Charlie drove pitchers to distraction by not swinging until he had two strikes on him, and still he remained one of the toughest men in the league to strike out. His lifetime batting average is .320.

Willis Hudlin, Cleveland right-hander from 1926 to 1940. A steady winner, he closed out with a 158–156 record.

For twenty years—1928 through 1947—right-hander Mel Harder curve-balled his way along for the Cleveland Indians. Mel's two biggest years came back to back in 1934 and 1935, when he was 20–12 and 22–11. Lifetime Mel stands at 223–186.

That's Washington Senators owner Clark Griffith on the right congratulating his shortstop, manager, and son-in-law Joe Cronin after the Senators clinched the pennant on September 21, 1933. All of Joe's distinctions notwithstanding, Griff sold him to the Red Sox a year later for a quarter of a million. Cronin played in the bigs from 1926 through 1945, batting .301 as one of the hardest-hitting shortstops in history. He later became president of the American League.

Washington's sharp-hitting pennant-winning outfield of 1933. Left to right: Fred Schulte, Goose Goslin, and Heinie Manush.

Luke Sewell, who came up with Cleveland in 1921 and stayed around for 20 years, catching for the Indians, Senators, and White Sox. He retired with a .259 career batting average.

Charles ("Buddy") Myer, second baseman from 1925 through 1941, most of it spent with Washington. Buddy won the batting crown in 1935 with a .349 average. Lifetime average: .303.

Earl Whitehill pitched for Detroit from 1923 through 1932, then went to Washington where his 22–8 record helped win a pennant in 1933. Earl pitched in the bigs until 1939, winning 218 and losing 185.

Alvin Crowder, known as "General." He pitched from 1926 to 1936 in the employ of the Senators, Browns, and Tigers. Alvin was 21–5 for the Browns in 1928, and 26–13 and 24–15 for the Senators in 1932 and 1933. His lifetime record is 167–115.

Outfielder Joe Vosmik joined the Indians in 1930 and gave them some hearty years, batting .341 in 1934 and .348 in 1935. Joe later played for the Browns and Red Sox and retired in 1944 with a .307 batting average.

Rookie shortstop Cecil Travis of the Washington Senators in 1933. He got five hits in his first game and never stopped hitting. He was well over .300 in seven of his first eight years, with a topper of .359 in 1941. Four years in the army cut the heart out of his career, and he retired in 1947 with a lifetime average of .314.

Detroit skipper Mickey Cochrane in 1936.

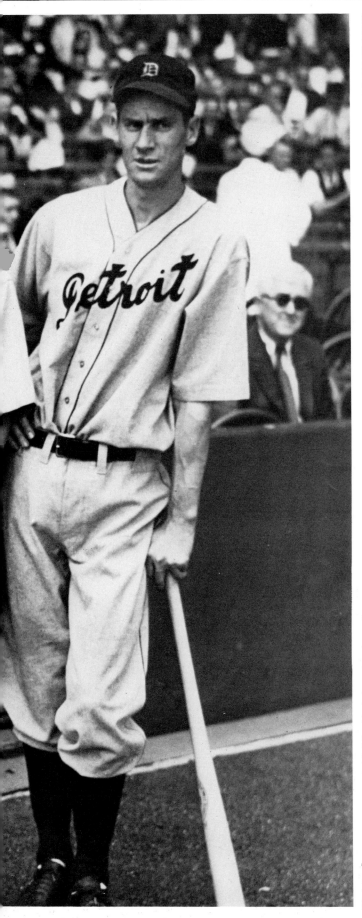

Hank Greenberg, one of baseball's all-time sluggers. Big Henry played with the Tigers from 1933 to 1946 (with four and a half years out for military service). He led four times in home runs, with a high of 58 in 1938, drove in 183 runs in 1937 and 170 in 1935, hit 63 doubles in 1934, and generally made life miserable for American League pitchers. He finished up with Pittsburgh in 1947. Lifetime batting average: .313. When he retired in 1947, Hank's 331 home runs placed him fifth on the all-time list behind Ruth, Foxx, Mel Ott, and Gehrig.

The infield that helped Detroit take pennants in 1934 and 1935. Left to right: Hank Greenberg, Charlie Gehringer, Billy Rogell, Marv Owen.

The mainstays of Detroit's 1934 pennant-winning pitching staff. Left to right: Eldon Auker, Fred Marberry, Tommy Bridges, and Lynwood ("Schoolboy") Rowe. Rowe was 24–8 that year, Bridges 22–11, while Auker and Marberry won 15 each.

The front-rank outfield of Detroit's 1934-35 pennant winners. Left to right: Goose Goslin, Jo-Jo White, Pete Fox. White batted .313 in 1934, his best year; Fox hit steadily throughout his career, which ran from 1933 through 1945, divided between the Tigers and Red Sox. Pete's lifetime is .298.

Luke Appling toiled at shortstop for the White Sox from 1930 to 1950, hitting .300 15 times. He led the league with .388 in 1936, highest average ever for a shortstop. He led again with .328 in 1943. Lifetime average: .310.

The erudite Moe Berg, a back-up catcher for the White Sox, Indians, Senators, and Red Sox from 1926 to 1939. Moe had a facility for languages. They said he could speak eleven languages and not hit in any of them. His lifetime mark is .243.

Henry ("Zeke") Bonura, first baseman with the White Sox and Senators in the 1930s. Zeke batted .330 and .345 for the White Sox in 1936–1937. He played from 1934 through 1940 and batted .307.

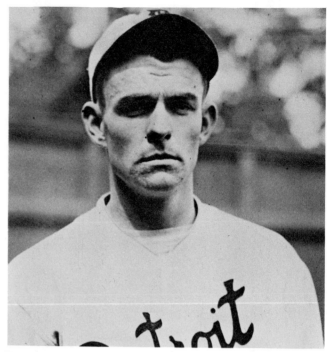

Billy Rogell, Detroit shortstop through the 1930s. Billy batted .267 for his 14-year career.

Tommy Bridges, right-handed curve-ball artist for the Tigers from 1930 to 1946. From 1934 to 1936 Tommy won 22, 21, and 23 games each year. Overall he was 194–138.

Three Philadelphia Athletic outfielders in 1936. Left to right: Wally Moses, Emil Mailho, Bob Johnson. Moses came up in 1935 and batted over .300 his first seven years. Wally played in the league until 1951, retiring with a .291 batting average. Mailho had a brief career. Johnson came up in 1933 and played his first ten years with the A's, driving in over 100 runs seven times. Bob retired in 1945 with a .296 lifetime average.

Mike ("Pinky") Higgins. Pinky played third for the A's, Red Sox, and Tigers from 1933 to 1946, hitting steadily all the way. His career average is .292. In 1938 he connected for 12 straight hits, a major-league record he shares with Walt Dropo.

Rollie Hemsley, big-league catcher from 1928 through 1947. He came to the American League from the National in 1933 and caught for the Browns and Indians through the 1930s. A noted tippler, Rollie nevertheless "could catch drunk better than most guys could sober," according to teammate Bob Feller. Rollie batted .262 lifetime.

Earl Averill, one of the American League's premier hitters in the 1930s. Earl played for Cleveland from 1929 to 1939, then was traded to Detroit. He retired in 1941. His biggest year was 1936, when he batted .378 and led with 232 hits. He batted .318 lifetime.

Cleveland's hard-hitting first baseman Hal Trosky. He swung a heavy bat for the Indians from 1933 through 1941, putting together his best year in 1936, when he batted .343, hit 42 home runs, and drove in 162 runs. He drove in over 100 runs six straight years and batted .330 or better four times. His lifetime average is .302.

Charlie ("Red") Ruffing. This great right-hander came to the big leagues with the Red Sox in 1924 and was dealt to the Yankees in 1930. He was the New York ace throughout the 1930s, winning 20 games four times. He pitched until 1947, leaving the game with a lifetime record of 273–225.

George ("Twinkletoes") Selkirk, the man who replaced Babe Ruth in right field for the Yankees. Selkirk played for New York from 1934 through 1942, hitting over .300 five times and averaging .290 for his career.

Two of the architects of the Yankee success. On the left, Manager Joe McCarthy, and General Manager Ed Barrow.

Joe DiMaggio in 1936.

Right-hander Irving ("Bump") Hadley came to the major leagues with Washington in 1926 and subsequently pitched for the White Sox, Browns, and Yankees before retiring in 1941 after short stints with the Giants and Athletics. For his 16 years in the big time, Bump showed a 161–165 record.

Robert ("Red") Rolfe, line-drive-hitting Yankee third baseman from 1934 through 1942. Red led with 213 hits in 1939, the year he recorded his career high .329 batting average. For his career Red was .289.

Vern Kennedy pitched in the big leagues from 1934 through 1945. His best year was 1936, when he was 21–9 with the White Sox. His lifetime record is 104–132.

Roger ("Doc") Cramer came up with the Athletics in 1929 and played until 1948, putting in time with the A's, Red Sox, Senators, and Tigers. An excellent center fielder with a steady bat, Doc batted .336 in 1932 and .332 in 1935. He collected 2,705 career hits and compiled a .296 batting average.

Joe DiMaggio and Bob Feller, the golden rookies of 1936.

Bob Feller in 1936. Ahead lay win totals of 24 (1939), 27 (1940), 25 (1941), 26 (1946) 20 (1947), 22 (1951), three no-hitters, twelve one-hitters, and a lifetime record of 266–142. He pitched from 1936 to 1956, losing four prime years to military service.

Harlond Clift played third base from 1934 through 1945, most of the time with the Browns. He had 34 home runs and 118 runs batted in in 1938. Lifetime average: .272.

Roy ("Beau") Bell came up with the Browns in 1935. In 1936 the right-handed-hitting outfielder batted .344 with 212 hits; the next year he batted .340 with a league-leading 218 hits and 51 doubles. He never repeated that success, later playing with Detroit and Cleveland, retiring in 1941 with a .297 average.

John ("Buddy") Lewis, fine outfielder and third baseman for Washington from 1935 to 1949. Like so many others, Buddy lost prime time to military service. He finished up with a .297 batting average.

Rick Ferrell, one of the fine catchers in American League history. He caught from 1929 to 1947, playing for the Browns, Red Sox (where he formed a battery with his brother Wes), and Senators. Lifetime batting average: .281.

For pitchers with 100 victories or more, the Yankees' right-hander Spud Chandler was the toughest to beat, with a .717 winning percentage based on a 109–43 record. Spud's peak seasons were 20–4 in 1943 and 20–8 in 1946. He pitched from 1937 through 1947.

Jeff Heath, hard-hitting outfielder for Cleveland from 1936 to 1945; later for the Senators, Browns, and Braves. Jeff hit .343 in 1938, .340 in 1941. He retired in 1949 with an average of .293.

Joe Kuhel, from 1930 to 1947 a first baseman for the Senators and White Sox. A slick glove, Joe batted .277 lifetime.

Mike Kreevich, stellar defensive center fielder with the White Sox from 1935 through 1941, later with the A's, Browns, and Senators. Mike's top year was 1939, when he batted .323. Lifetime he was .283.

First baseman George McQuinn spent his heyday years with the Browns from 1938 through 1945, batting .324 in 1938. He later played for the A's and Yankees, retiring in 1948 with a career mark of .276.

Lou Gehrig.

George Case, demon base-stealer of the Washington Senators from 1937 through 1945. One of baseball's all-time swifties, George led six times in swipes, with a high of 61 in 1943. Steady with the bat, George, an outfielder, posted a lifetime average of .282.

Emil ("Dutch") Leonard put in 20 big-league seasons from 1933 to 1953. Working in both leagues, the knuckle-balling right-hander pitched for Washington from 1938 to 1946, with a 20–8 record in 1939 his top year. Lifetime he was 191–181.

Lou Gehrig Appreciation Day, July 4, 1939, at Yankee Stadium.

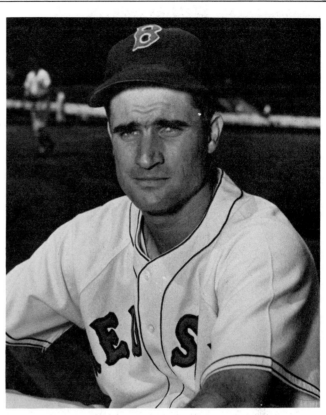

Jimmy Bloodworth, second baseman with Washington, Detroit, and several National League clubs from 1937 to 1951. He batted .248 lifetime.

Bobby Doerr, Boston's crack second baseman from 1937 to 1951. Bobby drove in over 100 runs in a season six times and six times led league second basemen in fielding. With a high of .325 in 1944, he had a lifetime batting average of .288.

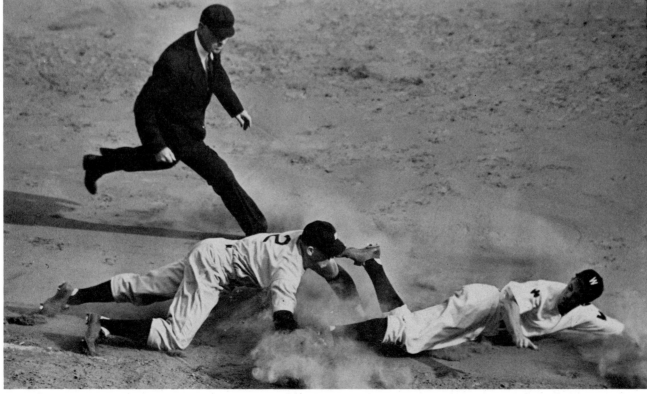

George Case stealing third base in a cloud of dust. The third baseman is New York's Red Rolfe.

Ted Williams, the most feared, respected, and admired hitter of his era. Among twentieth-century hitters, his lifetime .344 batting average is topped only by Cobb, Hornsby, and Joe Jackson. Losing five prime years in two separate tours of military service, he still hit 521 home runs, took six batting titles, and nine slugging titles. His lifetime .634 slugging average is second only to Ruth's.

Walt Judnich, St. Louis Browns outfielder from 1940 to 1947. He hit .313 in 1942 before going off to military service for three years. He swung a .281 lifetime bat.

Raymond ("Rip") Radcliff, a smooth-swinging outfielder for the White Sox, Browns, and Tigers from 1934 to 1943. Rip had four seasons over .325, with a .342 peak for the Browns in 1940. Lifetime average: .311.

It's April 16, 1940, and Bob Feller has just pitched the first opening day no-hitter in baseball history, against Chicago. Here Bob is being congratulated by teammates and assorted Cleveland brass.

Sam Chapman, power-hitting outfielder for the Athletics from 1938 to 1951. Sam batted .322 in 1941 before going off to war for four years. His career average is .266.

Ted Williams.

Dick Bartell was a 13-year National League veteran when the Tigers acquired him to play shortstop in 1940. He played a year, then returned to the National League, retiring in 1946. Lifetime average: .284.

George ("Birdie") Tebbetts, one of the league's steadier catchers with the Tigers, Red Sox, and Indians from 1936 to 1952. He batted .270 lifetime.

Barney McCosky joined the Tigers in 1939. A sweet-swinging center fielder, Barney batted .311, .340, .324, and .293 before going into the service. In 1946 he was traded to the Athletics and put up averages of .318, .328, and .326 before losing his stroke. He retired in 1953 with an average of .312.

Right-hander Sid Hudson worked for the Senators and Red Sox from 1940 to 1954, winning 104 and losing 152. His rookie year, when he won 17, was his best.

Power-hitter Rudy York came up as a catcher with the Tigers in 1934, was switched to first base a few years later and there played out his career until 1948. His 34 home runs and 118 runs batted in were tops in 1943. He was dealt to the Red Sox in 1946, then to the White Sox, and finished up with the A's, leaving with a .275 lifetime mark.

Hank Greenberg putting the ball in play.

Chet Laabs, outfielder with Detroit, the Browns, and Athletics from 1937 through 1947. His lifetime average is .262.

Between 1929 and 1953 it went like this for Bobo Newsom: the Dodgers, Cubs, Browns, Senators, Red Sox, Browns, Tigers, Senators, Dodgers, Browns, Senators, Athletics, Senators, Yankees, Giants, Senators, Athletics. Obviously, he was of equal parts charm and nuisance. But most of all, he could pitch, winning 20 in 1938, 1939, and 1940. When he picked up his final train ticket his record was 211–222.

Back from the war in 1946: Ted Williams and Joe DiMaggio.

5

And Then the War

All seemed normal and logical in that special universe called baseball for the next three years. After their unaccustomed dip in the chill waters of third place in 1940, Joe McCarthy's Yankees hauled themselves clear and raced through three straight comfortable and unthreatened pennant races. As if to atone in a hurry for their 1940 plunge from grace, the 1941 club battered the league apart and achieved the earliest clinching date in history, September 4, in their one hundred thirty-sixth game.

While all may have seemed normal and logical in baseball, there was a different brew in another part of the world. The spoilsports in Europe were at it again, unleashing armies and the grinding machines of destruction. This time the war was bigger and meaner and more dangerous, and once again the shadows began heaving across the ocean with ominous darkening. Reality hit baseball with sobering bluntness when early in the 1941 season one of the game's biggest cannoneers, Detroit's Hank Greenberg, entered the army.

If the front pages were ugly and glaring during that final prewar summer of 1941, the sports pages were throbbing with the kinds of thrills and excitement that serve to isolate the games we play and make them so special in our lives.

Appropriately, the action in baseball that was to rise above the decades to the heights of legend was generated by the right people. Joe DiMaggio hit a single on May 15 against the White Sox at Yankee Stadium and thus modestly launched one of sports' most memorable accomplishments. Not until the night of July 17 in Cleveland did a Yankee game pass without at least one DiMaggio hit. By the time it was over, the Yankee center fielder had fascinated the country with a 56-game hitting streak, during which he broke George Sisler's American League mark of 41, set in 1922, and Wee Willie Keeler's National League record of 44, set in the dark ages of 1897.

The streak, more than anything else, has served to symbolize the majesty of Joseph Paul DiMaggio: consistency, success upon success under ever-building pressure, a uniqueness, and ultimately a record that leaves him in splendid solitude. And when finally Joe was turned away empty on that July 17 night, it was only because one of the league's better gloves, Cleveland third baseman Ken Keltner, made two fine plays on DiMaggio-blistered ground balls. It was not a cold bat the Indians stopped that night, but rather one that was still smoking.

The other grand accomplishment of 1941 was Ted Williams' year-long assault on a .400 batting average. Williams' achievement has grown in immensity with the passing years; for in 1941 it was only 11 years since the previous .400 hitter, the Giants' Bill Terry with a .401 mark in 1930. After Williams' achievement, decade after decade has rolled by without anyone matching him.

The twenty-two-year-old Williams attained his gaudy heights with a power swing, launching 37 home runs. He did it with a flair, too, a flair worthy of, well, Ted Williams. On the season's final day, with a doubleheader scheduled against the Athletics, Ted was batting .3995—.400, to be exact. His manager, Joe Cronin, offered to sit him down. Ted said no, he would not back into it. So he played, determined to do it his way. And he did, gloriously. In the opener he went 4 for 5, collecting three singles and a home run. In the nightcap he singled and doubled in three trips. When it was over, he had cleared the hurdle with points to spare, ending with a mark of .406.

And so the 1941 season left behind two glittering neon-light numbers for baseball fans to conjure always: 56 and .406. Ten weeks

after the bats had been stacked, something else was burned into the minds of Americans, a month and a number: December 7.

The war was slow to encroach on baseball in 1942. Although Bob Feller joined the navy soon after Pearl Harbor, most of the other stars remained in place for one more year. Though DiMaggio dropped from .357 to .305, the Yankee firepower rolled easily to another pennant, helped by strong seasons from Charlie Keller and Joe Gordon. The Yankee farm system had by now coughed up shortstop Phil Rizzuto along with two more winning pitchers, 21-game winner Ernie Bonham and 15-game winner Hank Borowy, the newcomers picking up the tiring arms of veterans Red Ruffing and Lefty Gomez.

Williams continued poisoning the dreams of American League pitchers with a Triple Crown season of .356, 36 home runs, 137 runs batted in. For the fourth time in five years the Red Sox led in batting, but as usual their pitching kept them from October gravy, with only right-hander Cecil ("Tex") Hughson doing the job with a 22–6 season.

In Chicago, forty-one-year-old right-hander Ted Lyons celebrated his twentieth year with the White Sox by showing the youngsters how it was done. Lyons started 20 games, completed 20, winning 14 and losing 6, and leading the league with a 2.10 earned-run average. Satisfied with all that, he promptly enlisted in the marines.

During the next three seasons the major leagues, encouraged by President Roosevelt to keep going as a morale builder and source of diversion for the embattled country, had to scramble to keep filling the holes opened by departures to the military. Young and old, rejects and retreads, they came and played in the big leagues.

It took a world war for the St. Louis Browns to win their one and only pennant in 1944, a flag they won on the last day of the season. In 1945 the Tigers beat out the Senators in another photofinish race, winning on the last day on a ninth-inning grand slammer by Hank Greenberg, who had returned from the war in midseason.

It was in 1945 that a Browns outfielder named Pete Gray came to epitomize the desperate shortage of wartime talent. The twenty-eight-year-old Gray had lost his right arm in a childhood accident. Despite this handicap, he made it into pro ball and in 1945, after batting .333 for Memphis of the Southern Association, came up with the Browns. Gray got into 77 games and batted .218.

The first postwar season was one of exultant joy and booming profits, as baseball fans welcomed their heroes back in record numbers. Every club in the league with the exception of the lowly Browns and Athletics set new season highs in attendance, with the Yankees setting an all-time high with 2,265,512 spins of the turnstiles. Overall league attendance was 9,621,182, four million better than the previous record set the year before and nearly three quarters of a million more than the National League, which also enjoyed a record season.

It certainly was not an exciting pennant race that brought American League fans pouring into the ball parks. A heavy-hitting Boston Red Sox club ran off an early season 15-game winning streak to build up a big lead they never relinquished. Ted Williams returned from the naval air force to a typical Ted Williams season: .342 batting average, 38 home runs, 123 runs batted in. Shortstop Johnny Pesky batted .335, and center fielder Dominic DiMaggio .316.

Williams' fine season, along with a league-leading 44 home runs by Hank Greenberg, demonstrated that the mighty had not lost their edge while in service. Bob Feller, however, gave season-long evidence that despite four years in the navy he was mightier than ever. The Cleveland incomparable fired up an otherwise lackluster summer for Indian fans by his pursuit of the league strikeout record of 343 set by Rube Waddell in 1904. By the

time it was over, Feller had fanned 348 for a new record, although subsequent research through the box scores of 1904 credited Waddell with 349, all of which became academic when California's Nolan Ryan burned out 383 batters in 1973.

To get some measure of Feller's speed, only one other pitcher in the league fanned as many as 200 in 1946, and only nine others struck out as many as 100. In 1973, six pitchers besides Ryan struck out over 200 and altogether 30 pitchers whiffed over 100. Feller led American League pitchers in wins (26), complete games (36), innings (371), and shutouts (10). He also led in the number of games pitched (48), an intriguing league-leading statistic for a premier starting pitcher. Feller's 36 complete games were the most in the league since Walter Johnson's 38 in 1910, and no one has topped it since.

In 1947 the Yankees returned to the top, thanks to a 19-game winning streak in June and July that tore the race apart. The streak equaled the league record set by the 1906 White Sox. The year also saw Ted Williams become the first American Leaguer ever to win a second Triple Crown (only Rogers Hornsby had done it in the National League).

The Yankees' effort was spearheaded by a 19–8 season by Allie Reynolds, a hard-throwing right-hander obtained from Cleveland in a trade for second baseman Joe Gordon; and by outstanding relief pitching by left-hander Joe Page, a reformed starter and unreformed bon vivant who was all charm and hopping fast ball. DiMaggio swung a slightly slower bat than usual, hitting .315 with but 20 homers and 97 runs batted in, good enough to earn Joe an MVP from sportswriters, who must have thought Ted Williams was playing in another league that year.

All of this was interesting and exciting, but the league's most significant story of 1947 involved a twenty-three-year-old Cleveland second baseman (later outfielder) who broke into 29 games and batted but .156. His name was

Larry Doby and despite a later career of some resounding hitting, his lasting claim to fame lay in the fact of being the American League's first black player.

Jackie Robinson had integrated the National League with the Brooklyn Dodgers that April. Although most National League club owners continued to follow a philosophy of staunch conservatism for several years as far as blacks were concerned, they were a galaxy of veritable Nikolai Lenins compared to the American League bosses. (The St. Louis Browns did introduce blacks Henry Thompson and Willard Brown later in the season, but it seemed more of a gimmick than an act of principle. Both were gone the next year, with Thompson later resurfacing to have a fine career with the New York Giants.)

With the slow, steady infusion of the cream of black players into the National League, the erosion of American League supremacy had begun. Not until 1955, for instance, did the Yankees field their first black player, and the Boston Red Sox waited until 1959, three years after the retirement of Jackie Robinson, to integrate their team.

The Cleveland owner who brought Doby to the big leagues was Bill Veeck, a free-wheeling character with a genius for promotion, and, predictably, an anathema to his fellow club owners.

In 1948 Veeck's Indians took their first pennant since 1920 in the tightest pennant race in American League history—indeed, it ended in a tie between the Indians and Red Sox, necessitating the league's first pennant play-off ever. With the mighty Feller stumbling to a 19–15 season, the Cleveland pitching staff was headed by a rookie left-hander named Gene Bearden. Throwing a low-breaking knuckle ball, Bearden framed a fine 20–7 season. He was backed in strong fashion by converted outfielder Bob Lemon, who was 20–14 with ten shutouts. In midseason Veeck added to the staff one of the game's bona fide legends, the forty-one-year-old

Satchel Paige, long-time star of the Negro leagues, deprived of years of big-league glory because of the color barrier. With a 6–1 record and 2.47 ERA in 21 games, Paige had enough left to show what might have been.

At bat, the Indians were led by their dynamic shortstop-manager Lou Boudreau, who batted .355, outfielder Dale Mitchell, with a .336 average, and young Doby, who batted .301.

The Yankees finished 2½ games out despite Joe DiMaggio's 155 runs batted in and some solid stickwork by young Yogi Berra. Ted Williams and his .369 batting average led the Red Sox into the one-game play-off with Cleveland, but Bearden stopped them 8–3, thanks primarily to Boudreau who, in Red Smith's phrase, "managed like mad," hitting two home runs and two singles.

With the Yankees having taken just one pennant in the first three postwar seasons, the rest of the league was perhaps lulled into a false sense of security. Although light on pitching, the Red Sox seemed to have enough firepower to keep them in contention; Cleveland's pitching was formidable; the Tigers, with young players like George Kell, Vic Wertz, Hoot Evers, and Johnny Groth, looked like a coming team.

In 1949 Joe DiMaggio was thirty-four, Tommy Henrich thirty-six, while Charlie Keller had a bad back and was no longer a threat. In addition, the team had just hired a new manager who had a reputation for being a loser.

Ted Williams.

Joe DiMaggio.

Joe Gordon, the Yankees' flashy fielding, hard-hitting second baseman from 1938 to 1946, when he was traded to Cleveland. Joe's top year was 1942, when he batted .322 and was voted Most Valuable Player. He retired in 1950 with a .268 batting average.

Charlie Keller, the Yankees' long-balling left fielder from 1939 to 1949, when he was slowed down by back injuries. Charlie batted .334 in his rookie year. In 1941 he hit 33 home runs and had 122 runs batted in. Lifetime batting average: .286.

Right-hander Ernie Bonham was a big man, so his nickname was "Tiny." He was with the Yankees from 1940 through 1946, finishing up with Pittsburgh in 1949. Bonham's big year was 1942, when he was 21–5. His career stats read 103–72.

One of the most popular of all Yankee players was outfielder Tommy Henrich, called "Old Reliable" because of his clutch hitting. Tommy played for New York from 1937 to 1950, hitting 31 four-baggers in 1941. He batted .282 over his career.

Right-hander Hank Borowy broke in with the Yankees in 1942 with a 15–4 record, had several more winning seasons, and then was dealt to the Cubs midway through the 1945 season. He retired in 1951 with a 108–82 record.

Phil Rizzuto, crack Yankee shortstop from 1941 through 1956. In 1950 Phil's .324 batting average, 200 hits, and fine all-around play earned him the Most Valuable Player Award. His lifetime average is .273.

Ken Keltner, the Cleveland third baseman whose sharp glove helped put an end to DiMaggio's hitting streak in 1941. Ken played for the Indians from 1937 to 1949, with a lifetime average of .276.

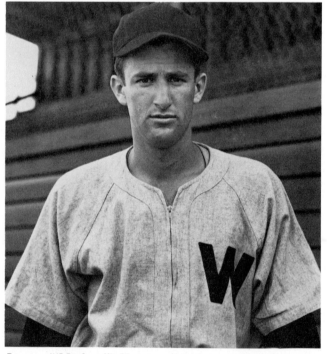

Johnny Murphy, superb Yankee relief pitcher from 1932 to 1946. He had a flashy 93–53 lifetime record.

James ("Mickey") Vernon, big-league first baseman from 1939 to 1960. Mickey spent the bulk of his career with Washington; he also played for the Indians and Red Sox, finishing up in the National League with the Braves and Pirates. He was the American League batting champion in 1946 with a .353 average and again in 1953 with .337. Lifetime he batted .286. Vernon played 2,237 games at first base, more than any other twentieth-century first baseman.

Three Detroit Tiger mainstays in 1941. Left to right: Barney McCosky, Rudy York, Charlie Gehringer.

Bob Feller being sworn into the United States Navy by former heavyweight champion Gene Tunney. The place is Chicago, the date December 8, 1941. Feller requested combat duty and got plenty of it in the Pacific as an antiaircraft gunner aboard the battleship *Alabama*.

Thornton Lee, big left-hander for the Indians and White Sox from 1933 to 1947. His best year was 1941, when he was 22–11 for the White Sox, a year he also led in ERA with 2.37. His final tally was 117–124.

Don Kolloway, second baseman for the White Sox and Tigers from 1940 to 1952. He batted .271 lifetime.

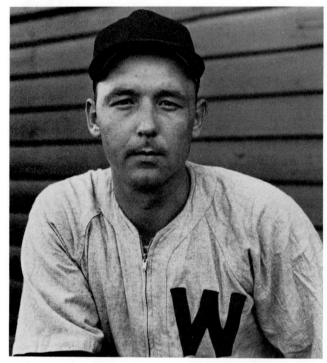

Playing with the Red Sox, Senators, and Browns from 1940 to 1949, outfielder Stan Spence had some good years. He hit .323 for Washington in 1942 with 203 hits, and .316 two years later. His career average is .282.

Lou Boudreau, Cleveland's great shortstop from 1939 to 1950, also its manager from 1942 to 1950. Lou won the batting championship in 1944 with a .327 average and helped win a pennant in 1948 with a .355 mark. He ended his playing career with the Red Sox in 1952 with a .295 lifetime batting average, later managing the Red Sox, Athletics, and Cubs.

Virgil ("Fire") Trucks, fast-balling right-hander for Detroit and four other clubs from 1941 to 1958. He won 19 for the Tigers in 1949 and 20 for the Browns and White Sox in 1953. In 1952 he pitched two no-hitters. Overall he was 177–135.

Vern Stephens, long-balling shortstop with the Browns and Red Sox from 1941 to 1952, when he was traded to the White Sox. He finished up with Baltimore in 1955. Vern led in runs batted in, in 1944 with 109, and again in 1949 and 1950 with the Red Sox with 159 and 144. He had 39 home runs in 1949. He batted .286 lifetime.

Home on leave in the summer of 1943, Seaman Phil Rizzuto drops in at Yankee Stadium for a visit with teammates Charlie Keller (left) and Bill Dickey.

Bob Muncrief pitched for the Browns from 1937 to 1947. Lifetime he was 80–82.

Right-hander Denny Galehouse pitched in the American League from 1934 to 1949, working for the Indians, Red Sox, and Browns, with an overall record of 109–118.

The ace of the St. Louis Browns staff in 1944 was right-hander Nelson Potter with a 19–7 record. Potter pitched in the majors from 1938 to 1949, doing the bulk of his work for the Athletics and Browns. He was 92–97 lifetime.

Right-hander Jack Kramer was one of the big winners on the 1944 pennant-winning Browns with a 17–13 record. After eight years with the Browns, he was dealt to the Red Sox in 1948 and posted an 18–5 season. He retired in 1951 with a 95–103 record.

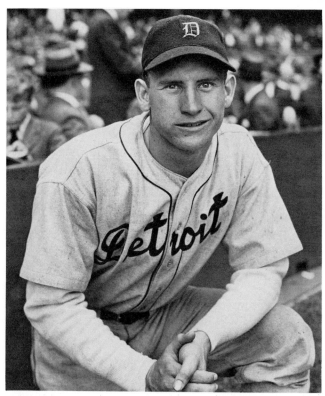

Right-hander Paul ("Dizzy") Trout pitched for Detroit from 1939 to 1952. He was 20–12 in 1943 and 27–14 in 1944, 170–161 overall.

Three winning pitchers on Boston's 1946 pennant winners. Left to right: southpaw Mickey Harris (17–9), right-handers Dave Ferriss (25–6) and Joe Dobson (13–7).

Pete Gray.

Cecil ("Tex") Hughson, Boston's superb pitcher from 1941 to 1949. Tex was 22–6 in 1942, 18–5 in 1944, and 20–11 in 1946, after which a bad arm cut into his career. He ended with a 96–54 record.

Left to right: Ted Williams, Johnny Pesky, and Dom DiMaggio of the 1946 Red Sox. Pesky played for the Red Sox and Tigers from 1942 to 1954, led the league in hits his first three years, and batted .307 lifetime. DiMaggio spent his entire career with the Red Sox, from 1940 to 1953, compiling a .298 average.

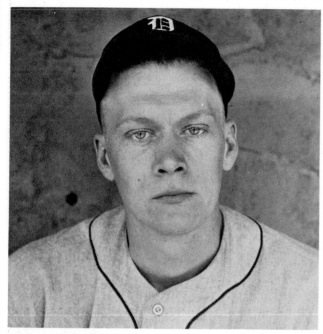

Walter ("Hoot") Evers, outfielder with Detroit and four other clubs from 1946 through 1956. Three times a .300 hitter, Hoot finished up with a .278 average.

Al Zarilla roamed the outfield for the Browns, Red Sox, and White Sox from 1943 to 1953. He hit .329 in 1948 for the Browns and .325 for the Red Sox in 1950. He was a lifetime .276 hitter.

The fiercely competitive Fred Hutchinson. He pitched for the Tigers from 1939 to 1953, winning 18 in 1947. Lifetime he was 95–71.

Bob Kennedy played infield and outfield for the White Sox, Indians, and three other clubs from 1939 to 1957. He batted .254 lifetime.

Outfielder Elmer Valo was a 20-year man, playing from 1940 to 1961, his first 14 years with the Athletics, and then with five other clubs. Five times a .300 hitter, Elmer ended up with a .282 lifetime mark.

Pete Suder (left) and Hank Majeski, second baseman and third baseman respectively on the Athletics in 1947. Pete was with the A's from 1941 to 1955, batting .249 for his career. Majeski, who hit .310 and drove in 120 runs for the A's in 1949, played for six big-league clubs from 1939 to 1955, batting .279 overall.

Pat Mullin, Detroit outfielder from 1940 to 1953. Lifetime average: .271.

Lawrence Peter ("Yogi") Berra, a Yankee rookie in 1947.

Lefty Joe Page was with the Yankees from 1944 to 1950. He helped them to pennants in 1947 and 1949 with some dazzling relief pitching. He retired with a 57–49 record.

Larry Doby. He gave Cleveland some fine years between 1947 and 1955, batting .326 in 1950 and leading in home runs in 1952 (32) and 1954 (32). He later played for the White Sox and Tigers, retiring in 1959 with a .283 batting average.

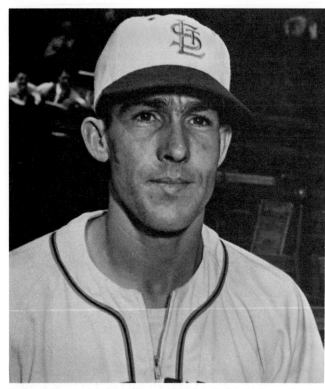

A lot of people thought outfielder Paul Lehner had a natural stroke and would be a star. But it never happened. He came up with the Browns in 1946, then shuffled through the league until retiring in 1952. His best year was 1950, when he batted .309 for the Athletics. Lifetime he stands at .257.

Henry Thompson played briefly for the Browns in 1947, then went on to a fine career for the New York Giants from 1949 to 1956, batting .267.

Four of the solid men behind Cleveland's 1948 drive to the pennant. Left to right: Joe Gordon, Ken Keltner, Dale Mitchell, Lou Boudreau.

Satchel Paige. Paige pitched for Cleveland and the Browns from 1948 to 1953, leaving with a 28–31 life-time record, after coming to the major leagues at the age of forty-two.

Knuckle-balling southpaw Gene Bearden gave the Indians one memorable year in 1948, winning 20, losing 7, and leading in ERA with 2.43. He never came close to that, pitching for five more teams before leaving the big leagues in 1953 with a 45–38 record.

Taft Wright, shown here with the Athletics in 1949, his last year in the majors. Playing with the Senators and White Sox from 1938 to 1948, Wright had some fine years, including .350 in his rookie year, .337 in 1940, and .333 in 1942. Lifetime average: .311.

Right-hander Ray Scarborough came up with Washington in 1942 and pitched for them until 1950, when he began making the rounds of the league, pitching for four more teams. Ray's best was 15–8 with the Senators in 1948. He was 80–85 lifetime.

Joe DiMaggio.

It is 1951 and the Yankees have one center fielder going and one coming. Joe DiMaggio (left) and Mickey Mantle.

6

The Yankees, etc.

It was true that the clubs Casey Stengel managed in the National League—Brooklyn from 1934 through 1936 and Boston from 1938 through 1943—were lasting symbols of ineptitude. Stengel's problem was he had wit, personality, and charm; he was able to "smile through." Because he seemed to accept his fate without ranting and raging, and indeed with quips, he was regarded by some as a loser and a clown. But behind that craggy face and between those fanned-out ears lay one of baseball's shrewdest minds.

When Stengel took over the Yankees he launched for himself a second career that in retrospect looks almost schizoid. The hapless loser became the game's most prodigious managerial winner. Beginning in 1949, the Yankees shocked the league with five consecutive pennants, an unprecedented accomplishment.

None of the flags, with the exception of the last, were particularly easy. In 1949 the Yankees, playing all season long with an injury-riddled team—DiMaggio did not play his first game until late June—edged out a powerhouse Red Sox team on the last day of the season on a clutch pitching performance by Vic Raschi, Stengel's ace. The Sox, managed by Joe McCarthy, outslugged the Yankees in every department, but came up a game short.

Platooning, manipulating, rebuilding as he went, Stengel won in 1950 by three games over Detroit; by five in 1951 over Cleveland and Al Lopez's magnificent pitching staff; by two over Cleveland in 1952; by eight and one half over Cleveland in 1953.

Stengel did it with an aging DiMaggio, with the unlikely looking but slugging

Yogi Berra, with Phil Rizzuto, Hank Bauer, Gene Woodling, Jerry Coleman, Bobby Brown, Gil McDougald, Billy Martin, Joe Collins, National League veteran Johnny Mize, and others. He did it with an array of superb pitchers—Vic Raschi, Allie Reynolds, Eddie Lopat, Tommy Byrne, Johnny Sain, and a product of New York's sandlots named Whitey Ford, who became the most successful of all Yankee pitchers.

The Yankees kept on winning despite the loss to retirement in 1951 of the preeminent Yankee, Joe DiMaggio. For years the Yankees had been giving object lessons in perpetuating a dynasty: a Ruth was replaced by a DiMaggio, a Crosetti by a Rizzuto, a Dickey by a Berra. And now even the peerless DiMaggio was to be replaced in center by one of the most abundantly gifted ballplayers of all time.

The Oklahoma-born Mickey Mantle (named after his father's favorite ballplayer Mickey Cochrane, whose first name was really Gordon) could hit with devastating power from either side of the plate, outrun rabbits and Rolls-Royces, and throw with the might of a howitzer. He was tough, he was inspirational, and he was a winner. Blond, built like a halfback, with the smile and boyish good looks of an American small-time *beau ideal*, Mantle put together a glittering 18-year career that elevated him into the Ruth-Gehrig-DiMaggio pantheon of Yankee untouchables. If not for a career-long history of injuries, he might have rewritten the record book entirely.

Whitey Ford, a canny left-hander with an assortment of tough-to-hit breaking pitches and the guile and confidence of the city slicker that he was, rose through the farm system, joined the club in late June of 1950, won his first nine decisions, then went off to two years in the military.

Stengel's most tenacious pursuer throughout the 1950s was Al Lopez, managing Cleveland and later Chicago. Lopez finished second seven times to Stengel's Yankees. The hall-mark of Al's Cleveland teams was pitching. In 1951, the year he took the club over from Boudreau, Al had three 20-game winners in Feller, Mike Garcia, and Early Wynn, plus a 17-game winner in Lemon. In 1952 Lemon, Wynn, and Garcia each won over 20. In 1953 Lemon won 21, Garcia 18, Wynn 17.

In 1954 Lopez and his Indians put together a herculean, record-breaking effort and finally overhauled the Yankees. It took an unrelenting effort, too, because Stengel's five-time champions had their biggest year ever under their sixty-four-year-old skipper, winning 103 games.

In 1954 Cleveland set an all-time American League record with 111 wins, breaking by one the mark set by the 1927 Yankees. Pitching was the club's calling card, and the staff was one of the finest ever put together. It was topped by 23-game winners Lemon and Wynn, 19-game winner Garcia, and 15-game winner Art Houtteman. The veteran Bob Feller turned in his last winning season with a 13–3 record. In addition to this outstanding brigade of starters, Lopez had two stoppers performing nobly out of the bullpen all year long—lefty Don Mossi and righty Ray Narleski. Otherwise it was hardly a memorable club, certainly not one built to set a victory record. Second baseman Bobby Avila batted a league-leading .341, Larry Doby led in home runs and runs batted in, and third baseman Al Rosen provided some sock. But beyond these worthies there was little to fear in the lineup that won 111 games.

The 1954 season saw the first franchise shift in the American League since 1903, when Baltimore had been dropped to make room for New York. Now, half a century later, the Orioles were back, replacing the St. Louis Browns, for years a near-comatose franchise. Only eleven times had the Browns finished in the first division. In the 1930s their season's attendance had three times dipped below 100,000. In 1953, their last year in St. Louis, they drew under 300,000. In 1954, their first season in Baltimore, they drew over one million, a statistic that stuck in the eyes of club owners like pieces of mica.

The next club to declare the past null and void was the Philadelphia Athletics. Connie Mack had finally retired in 1950 at the age of eighty-seven. A few years later the Mack family sold out their interests in the club to a man named Arnold Johnson, who had one foot out the door even as he was signing the papers. Johnson promptly moved the heirs of Rube Waddell, Eddie Collins, Lefty Grove, Jimmie Foxx, and others out to Kansas City, hitherto a New York Yankee farm club. (Some cynics would say a few years later that a New York Yankee farm club it remained, when Johnson began shipping all of his good players to New York.) The reason for the move to Kansas City was disappearing customers—the A's drew just 304,000 lonely souls in their last Philly go-around. When they jacked that up by a million in their first year in Kansas, owners of other withering franchises began reaching for the nearest atlas.

In 1955 Stengel won several fewer games than in 1954, but Al Lopez won 18 fewer, and the Yankees had slipped the leash again, off on a tear that would net them another four flags in a row before they could be hauled down. Most of these pennants were won with relative ease, and each time the man enjoying the view from second place was the patient, imperturbable Lopez.

A realist, Lopez probably felt that second place was honorable and all to be hoped for, for these were smooth-running Yankee machines, these 1955–1958 clubs. Mickey Mantle was at the head of the class now, turning baseballs into mere dots in the sky with prodigious blasts from both sides of the plate. In 1955 the Oklahoma Kid led with 37 home runs, but that was just a warm-up for a Triple Crown season in 1956, with 52 dots in the sky, 130 runs batted in, and a .353 batting average.

Mantle's chief cohorts in these summer romps were Bill Skowron, the team's best first baseman since Gehrig; Gil McDougald, Andy Carey, Hank Bauer, Billy Martin, Elston Howard, the estimable Mr. Berra (thanks to a lethal bat, a penchant for malapropisms, and baseball's most priceless nickname, one of America's best-known citizens), Bobby Richardson, Tony Kubek, and pitchers Whitey Ford, Johnny Kucks, Tom Sturdivant, Bob Turley, Don Larsen, Bobby Shantz, Art Ditmar, and a relief pitcher with poor eyesight and a fearsome fast ball named Ryne Duren. Most of these were graduates of an endlessly productive Yankee farm system, while some of the others arrived on the shuttle from Kansas City, where the Yankees sent their ailing arms and tiring bodies in exchange for fresh ones.

While the Yankees were committing mayhem on the rest of the league, there were other bright young stars laboring in the shadows. Cleveland brought up the niftiest left arm since Grove's. It belonged to young Herb Score. The twenty-two-year-old youngster with the greyhound build and torrid fast ball broke in, in 1955, with a rookie strikeout record of 245. He got better the next year and was getting even better when in May 1957 a line drive whistled from the bat of Gil McDougald struck him in the eye and for all intents and purposes brought a Hall of Fame career to a heartbreaking end. Just a few weeks before, Boston's Tom Yawkey had offered the Indians a million dollars cash for Score. This was a time when, as the insolvent like to say, a million dollars was a lot of money.

The White Sox had pepper-pot second baseman Nelson Fox and lefty Billy Pierce; Detroit had line-drive-hitting shortstop Harvey Kuenn and one of the finest of ballplayers in right fielder Al Kaline, a batting champ in 1955 at the almost beardless age of twenty, and right-hander Frank Lary who had a knack for beating the Yankees (he was 28–13 lifetime against them); and Washington was about to turn loose a bristling mass of muscles named Harmon Killebrew who would go on to hit 573 home runs.

Meanwhile, up in Boston, the Red Sox had a thirty-six-year-old outfielder named Ted Williams who was still doing what he had been doing since 1939. He was "Teddy Ballgame" now, last of the old titans, a walking legend, still flawless of swing and relentlessly independent of spirit. In 1955 he batted .356 in an injury-curtailed year, in 1956 he popped away to a .345 average. In 1957, at the age of thirty-eight, he startled everyone with a monumental .388 batting average and a monstrous .731 slugging average, a figure topped in American League history only by Ruth, Gehrig, Foxx, and Theodore himself. Williams' .388 deprived Mantle of a second batting crown, Mickey thundering away at .365.

In 1958 Williams dropped to .328, but that was still good enough to carry away his sixth and final batting title at the age of thirty-nine. Teddy's outfield buddy, Jackie Jensen, led in runs batted in with 122 in addition to hitting 35 home runs. Jensen, the league's most prolific RBI man at the time, had come up with the Yankees, been deemed superfluous and been traded. That the Yankees could dispense with such talent was intimidating; that they never missed it was downright scary. (The New Yorkers were having a tough enough time trying to fit .314-hitting Elston Howard into the lineup.)

In 1958 the league's only 20-game winner was New York's Bob Turley, a right-hander with an M-1 arm. Turley and righty Don Larsen had been obtained a few years before from Baltimore for a battalion of players the Orioles hoped to build around. It didn't work. Eventually, the Orioles built their dynasty, but it came out of their own farm system. Already in place at third base was a human vacuum cleaner named Brooks Robinson, an engaging twenty-one-year-old with a Houdini glove, but then still light of stick. When skipper Paul Richards wanted to farm Robinson out to have

the youngster work on his hitting, the Oriole pitchers came to Richards almost en masse with the same message: "We don't care if he never gets a hit. Just please leave him in there."

In 1959 young Harmon Killebrew played his first full season and surprised everyone with 42 home runs, enough four-baggers to earn him a tie at the top with Cleveland's own young buster, Rocky Colavito. Detroit's Harvey Kuenn helped sustain a Tiger tradition by leading the league with a .353 average—it was Detroit's twenty-first batting title in 59 years (a dozen of them belonging to Mr. Cobb).

The big news in the American League in 1959, however, was not so much who won the pennant as who did not. The Yankees didn't. Al Lopez, that sly old model of patience and perseverance, now lurking in ambush in Comiskey Park, sent an unlikely White Sox club scampering and hustling through the league to capture the club's first title since the shady 1919 gang.

Lopez did it in Chicago the same way he had done it in Cleveland—pitching. Leading a fine mound array was one of Al's old Cleveland aces, Early Wynn. Closing in on 300 lifetime victories, the thirty-nine-year-old Wynn had his last great season with a 22–10 record. He was backed up on the mound by Bob Shaw and Billy Pierce, plus an outstanding bullpen duo of Gerry Staley and Turk Lown.

The White Sox's keystone combination of second baseman Nelson Fox and shortstop Luis Aparicio was one of the best. Fox was a pestiferous competitor, a nonstop hustler. For ten consecutive years (1952–1961) he led second basemen in putouts; between 1951 and 1960 his batting average never dipped below .285. Seven times he led in fielding, four times in hits, eight times in singles, eleven times in fewest strikeouts.

Aparicio, in his fourth big-league season in 1959, was as accomplished a shortstop as ever played in the major leagues. For eight straight seasons the flashy Venezuelan led in fielding, and he set a record by leading in stolen bases his first nine years in the bigs. His top total was 57, modest by later-year standards; but Luis frequently outstole entire ball clubs, the way Ruth used to outhomer them.

After some early season stumbling in 1960, Stengel's Yankees finally got squared away and began their pennant trot. A young, pitching-rich Oriole team nipped at their heels through much of the summer, but the Yankees finished the season in high style, winning their last 15 in a row and taking the pennant by eight games.

In a season in which their pitching fell down—Art Ditmar's 15 wins led the staff—the Yankee hitting was impressive. Mantle hit 40 home runs. Right behind him was the Yankees' most recent acquisition from the obliging Kansas City club—Roger Maris. A left-handed hitter with a stroke custom-made for the Stadium, Maris belted 39 big ones, followed by Bill Skowron's 26. The team hit 193 home runs, at that time the seventh highest total ever.

The 1960 season marked the farewell appearances of two of the league's dominant figures. After batting .254 in 1959, many assumed the forty-year-old Ted Williams was through. Teddy Ballgame felt otherwise. Giving it one more go in 1960, he went out in proper fashion, batting .316 and hitting 29 home runs in just 310 at bats, including one last heroic belt in his last major-league at bat. Ted circled the bases as a Fenway Park crowd stood and applauded, refused to tip his cap, and disappeared into the dugout. Next stop: Cooperstown.

The other retirement was definitely not voluntary. After losing a pulsing World Series to Pittsburgh, Yankee Manager Casey Stengel was fired, ostensibly for being too old. ("I'll never make the mistake of being seventy years old again," the disgruntled Stengel said.) Af-

ter winning ten pennants in twelve years, the old man was gone, only to come back in 1962 as skipper on the newly formed New York Mets. Casey's replacement was Yankee coach Ralph Houk. Houk was a sound baseball man, admired and respected by his players, a splendid manager. The club he was taking over, however, was to prove so mighty it could probably have won without a manager.

Casey Stengel in 1949.

Tommy Byrne, New York's sometimes erratic fast-balling lefty. Tommy was with the Yankees from 1943 to 1951 and again from 1954 to 1957, in between being exiled to the Browns, White Sox, and Senators. He was 16–5 for Stengel in 1955.

Outfielder Gene Woodling played for six big-league teams from 1943 to 1962, most notably with the Yankees from 1949 to 1954. Five times a .300 hitter, his career mark is .284.

Popular Yankee outfielder Hank Bauer. He played for New York from 1948 to 1959, finishing up with Kansas City in 1961. Hank batted .320 in 1950, .277 overall.

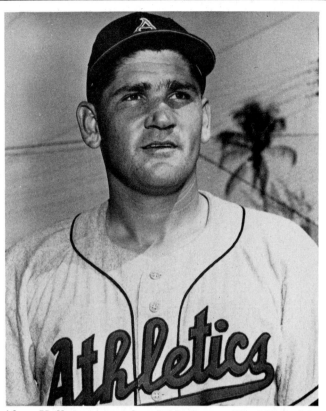

Mel Parnell, the Red Sox' crack southpaw from 1947 to 1956. He was 25–7 in 1949, 21–8 in 1953, and 123–75 overall.

Alex Kellner gave the Athletics a 20–12 rookie season in 1949 and never topped it. Pitching until 1959, he ended with a 101–112 record.

A serious beaning ended second baseman Cass Michaels' career in 1954 after 12 years, most of them spent with the White Sox. He batted .262 lifetime.

Right-hander Joe Coleman pitched for the A's, Orioles, and Tigers from 1942 to 1955, winning 52 and losing 76. His son, also named Joe, pitched in the big leagues in the 1960s and 1970s.

St. Louis Browns outfielders Roy Sievers (left) and Dick Kokos. Sievers played from 1949 to 1965, turning in his biggest years with Washington in the mid-1950s. He led with 42 home runs in 1957. Lifetime he hit 318 homers and batted .267. Kokos was with the Browns from 1948 to 1953, batting .263 lifetime.

Left-hander Lew Brissie pitched for the A's and Indians from 1947 to 1953. His top year was 1949, when he was 16–11. His career record is 44–48.

Four Tigers showing off their lumber in 1950, the year the club made an unsuccessful run for the pennant. Left to right: third baseman George Kell, outfielders Hoot Evers, Vic Wertz, Johnny Groth.

A clutch of Detroit Tiger pitchers in spring training in 1949. Left to right: Dizzy Trout, Ted Gray, Art Houtteman, Marv Grissom, Virgil Trucks, Saul Rogovin.

Ted Williams (left) with Red Sox teammates Billy Goodman (center) and Walt Dropo. Billy won a batting championship in 1950 with a .354 average. Playing from 1947 through 1962, Billy finished with an even .300 batting average. Dropo, playing with five different teams from 1949 to 1961, had his biggest year in 1950 with the Red Sox, when he drove in a league-leading 144 runs. He batted .270 lifetime.

George Kell, one of the greatest of all third base-men. He won the batting title in 1949 with a .343 average, then hit .340 the next year and led with 218 hits and 56 doubles. Playing from 1943 to 1957 with five different teams, he batted over .300 nine times, .306 lifetime.

Cleveland's Dale Mitchell, a .300-hitting outfielder from 1946 to 1956. He batted .336 in 1948, .312 lifetime.

Casey Stengel with his formidable trio of starters. Left to right: Allie Reynolds, Vic Raschi, Eddie Lopat. Reynolds, who pitched from 1942 to 1954, was 182–107 lifetime. Raschi pitched from 1946 to 1955 and was 132–66 lifetime. Lopat, who came to the Yankees from the White Sox in 1948, pitched from 1944 to 1955 and was 166–112 lifetime.

Left to right: Nelson Fox, Orestes ("Minnie") Minoso, and Eddie Robinson of the 1951 White Sox. Fox played from 1947 to 1965 and batted .288; Minoso was active from 1949 to 1964, with a .298 lifetime average; while Robinson played from 1946 to 1957 and batted .268.

Athletics Manager Jimmy Dykes (center) with outfielders Dave Philley (left) and Gus Zernial in 1951. A journeyman who played with eight teams from 1941 to 1962, Philley, who was a most productive pinch hitter toward the end of his career, batted .270. Zernial played from 1949 to 1959 and led with 33 home runs in 1951. He batted .265 lifetime.

Luke Easter, Cleveland's large-sized first baseman from 1949 to 1954. A power hitter, Luke twice drove in over 100 runs and hit 31 home runs in 1952. Career average: .274.

First baseman Ferris Fain took back-to-back batting titles with the A's in 1951–1952 with averages of .344 and .327. He played from 1947 to 1955, mostly with the Athletics. Lifetime average: .290.

Vic Raschi. He won 21 games in each of 1949, 1950, and 1951.

Allie Reynolds. His best year in New York was 1952, when he was 20–8 and led in ERA, strikeouts, and shutouts. In 1951 he pitched two no-hitters.

Chico Carrasquel, Chicago White Sox shortstop from 1950 to 1955. He later played for Cleveland, Kansas City, and Baltimore, retiring in 1959 with a .258 batting average.

Ned Garver, fine right-hander with the Browns, Tigers, and Athletics from 1948 to 1961. In 1951 he was 20–12 with a Browns team that finished in last place. Lifetime record: 129–157.

Johnny Lipon. He played shortstop for the Tigers and two other clubs from 1942 to 1953. He batted .259 lifetime.

The Athletics' Bobby Shantz (left) and Harry Byrd in spring training at West Palm Beach, Florida, in March 1953. The year before, Shantz was American League MVP with a 24–7 record and Byrd was Rookie of the Year with a 15–15 record.

Vic Wertz, power-hitting outfielder and first baseman for five American League teams from 1947 to 1963. He drove in over 100 runs five times, with a high of 133 in 1949. He was a .277 lifetime batter.

Johnny Mize showing off the ball that became his two thousandth major-league hit in 1953. Mize, a long-time National League veteran, was a part-time first baseman and lethal pinch hitter for the Yankees from 1949 through 1953. Lifetime average: .312.

Hard-throwing right-hander Bob Porterfield came up with the Yankees in 1948. He had his best season for Washington in 1953, when he was 22–10. He pitched until 1959, retiring with an 87–97 record.

Al Rosen, Cleveland third baseman from 1947 to 1956. He was the league's MVP in 1953, when he batted .336 and led with 43 home runs and 145 runs batted in. He was a lifetime .285 hitter.

Bobby Avila, Cleveland second baseman from 1949 through 1958 and American League batting champion in 1954 with a .341 average. Lifetime he batted .281.

Al Lopez and his three great starters in 1954. Left to right: Lopez, Mike Garcia, Bob Lemon, Early Wynn. Garcia, twice a 20-game winner, pitched from 1948 to 1961, winning 142 and losing 97. Lemon pitched from 1946 to 1958, was seven times a 20-game winner, and finished with a 207–128 record. Wynn pitched from 1939 to 1963 and was 300–244, winning 20 or more five times.

Don Mossi, Cleveland's left-handed bullpen ace in 1954. Don pitched from 1954 to 1965, mostly with Cleveland and Detroit. Lifetime record: 101–80.

Ray Narleski. The right-handed side of Cleveland's dynamic 1954 bullpen pitched big-league ball from 1954 through 1959, compiling a 43–33 record.

Gus Zernial, one of the league's big belters in the early 1950s. Gus popped 33 long ones for the White Sox and A's in 1951 and 42 in 1953. He played from 1949 to 1959, batting .265.

Bob Keegan pitched for the White Sox from 1953 to 1958. His lifetime record is 40–36. One of his wins was a no-hitter against Washington in 1957.

Whitey Ford, the Yankees' peerless left-hander from 1950 to 1967. In 1961 he was 25–4, in 1963 24–7. Overall he was 236–106. Among pitchers with 200 or more victories, his .690 winning percentage is the highest of all time.

Jackie Jensen, outfielder with the Yankees, Senators, and Red Sox from 1950 to 1961. Playing the bulk of his career with Boston, Jensen knocked in over 100 runs five times, leading the league in 1955, 1958, 1959. Lifetime batting average: .279.

Jimmy Piersall, colorful, talented, and controversial outfielder with the Red Sox and four other teams from 1950 to 1967. His best year was 1961 with Cleveland, when he batted .322. Lifetime he batted .272.

The man making the midair peg to first is Detroit's Harvey Kuenn, after forcing Philadelphia's Bob Trice at second. The action took place in June 1954.

Yogi Berra showing off the plaques he was given as the American League's Most Valuable Player in 1951 and 1954. He won another one in 1955.

Harvey Kuenn. A line-drive-hitting shortstop for the Tigers from 1952 to 1959, Harvey took the batting title in 1959 with a .353 average. He also led in hits four times. He was traded to Cleveland in 1960 and then played in the National League until 1966. He had a .303 lifetime average.

Al Kaline, one of Detroit's all-time greats. He played from 1953 through 1974, winning a batting title in 1955 with a .340 average, collecting a career total of 3,007 hits, including 399 home runs. Lifetime batting average: .297.

Ray Boone, shortstop and third baseman with Cleveland and Detroit and four other teams from 1948 to 1960. He was the RBI leader with Detroit in 1955 (tied with Jackie Jensen). He had a career batting average of .275.

Right-hander Frank Lary was a Detroit ace from 1955 to 1964, when arm trouble slowed him down. He won 21 in 1956 and 23 in 1961. Overall he was 128–116.

Left-hander Billy Hoeft joined the Tigers as a bonus baby in 1952 and pitched for them until 1959. He worked for five more teams before retiring in 1966 with a 97–101 record. He was a 20-game winner in 1956.

That's rookie shortstop Luis Aparicio of the White Sox being studied by skipper Marty Marion, a great short-stop himself with the Cardinals in the 1940s. Luis came up in 1956, played until 1973 with the White Sox, Orioles, and Red Sox, and batted .262. Aparicio's 2,581 games at shortstop is the all-time record for the position.

Mickey Mantle. A Yankee from 1951 through 1968. Lifetime figures: 536 home runs, .298 batting average.

The Yankees' Gil McDougald reading an account of Herb Score's injury. It was McDougald's line drive that struck the great Cleveland lefty in the eye. Gil was a Yankee from 1951 to 1960, playing second, short, and third with equal skill. His career average is .276.

Cleveland's Herb Score being congratulated by catcher Jim Hegan after defeating Baltimore in September 1955.

Early Wynn. One of the rarest of pitching breeds—the 300-game winner.

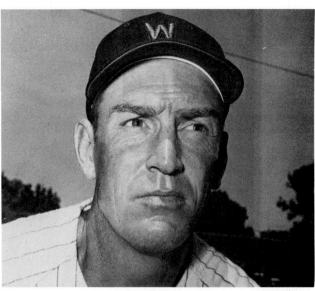

Frank Bolling, second baseman with the Tigers and Braves from 1954 to 1966. He was a .254 lifetime hitter.

Jim Bunning, Tiger ace from 1956 through 1963, when he was dealt to the National League, where he pitched until 1971. He was 20–8 with Detroit in 1957, his best year. Lifetime he checks in at 224–184.

Outfielder Jim Lemon, distance hitter for the Senators and Twins from 1954 to 1963. His biggest year was 1960, when he launched 38 long ones. He batted .262 lifetime.

Elston Howard of the New York Yankees. Joining the Yankees as an outfielder, Elston eventually replaced Yogi Berra behind the plate and remained with the Yankees until 1967, finishing up with the Red Sox the next year. He was voted the league's Most Valuable Player in 1963. He was a .274 lifetime hitter.

A picture of Ted Williams autographing a picture of Ted Williams. The year is 1960, Ted's last as an active player.

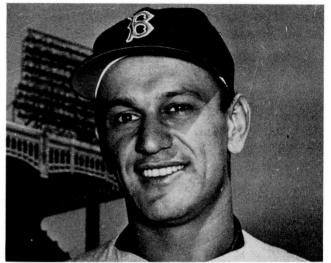

Frank Malzone, Boston's steady third baseman from 1955 to 1965. He finished up with California in 1966. Lifetime batting average: .274.

Rocky Colavito, home run-hitting outfielder with Cleveland, Detroit, Kansas City, and three other clubs from 1955 to 1968. Rocky hit over 40 home runs three times and drove in over 100 runs six times. On June 10, 1959, he hit four home runs in a game. Rocky had 374 home runs lifetime and a .266 batting average.

Bob Turley. They called him "Bullet Bob" because that's what he threw. Obtained by the Yankees from Baltimore in 1955, Bob's big year was 1958, when he was 21–7 and was the Cy Young Award winner. He pitched until 1963, retiring with a 101–85 record.

Vic Power, one of the flashiest gloves ever around first base. He came up with the Athletics in 1954 and later put in service with Cleveland and Minnesota among others before retiring in 1965 with a batting mark of .284.

Cleveland Indians brain trust conferring at the club's spring camp in Tucson in March 1958. Left to right: Coach Eddie Stanky, Manager Bobby Bragan, General Manager Frank Lane.

Acknowledged as one of the finest baseball minds of his time, Paul Richards managed the White Sox and Orioles from 1951 to 1961.

The Yankees' awesomely fast relief pitcher Ryne Duren. His heyday was the late 1950s. Ryne pitched for seven teams from 1954 to 1965, posting a 27–44 record but fanning 630 batters in 589 innings.

Right-hander Paul Foytack, Detroit fast baller from 1953 to 1963. He was 86–87 lifetime.

Right-handers Jerry Walker (left) and Jack Fisher of the Baltimore Orioles in 1959. Walker pitched for three clubs from 1957 to 1964 and was 37–44. Fisher, working for five teams from 1959 to 1969, was 86–139 lifetime. A better pitcher than his record indicates, Jack was stuck with a lowly New York Mets team for four years.

Sherman Lollar caught from 1946 to 1963, the last 12 of those years with the White Sox. Through 18 big-league seasons he batted .264.

Billy Pierce, crack southpaw for the White Sox from 1949 to 1961. He was a 20-game winner in 1956 and 1957. After finishing up with the San Francisco Giants in 1964, Billy's record stood at 211–169.

Jim Landis, outstanding center fielder on the pennant-winning 1959 White Sox. Most of Jim's 1957–1967 major-league career was spent in Chicago. He batted .247 lifetime.

A big-league pitcher from 1950 to 1965, Dick Donovan had some fine years with the White Sox and Indians, winning 20 for Cleveland in 1962. Lifetime he was 122–99.

Jim Rivera, hustling outfielder for the Browns and White Sox from 1952 to 1961. Lifetime average: .256.

A National League castoff whom the White Sox picked up in 1958, Omar ("Turk") Lown gave the Sox some first-class bullpen work in their 1959 pennant victory. Pitching from 1951 to 1962, Turk was 55–61.

Harmon Killebrew. One of baseball's all-time big boppers. He played from 1954 to 1975, all but the last year with the Washington Senators–Minnesota Twins. He led six times in home runs, with peaks of 49 in 1964 and 1969, and nine times drove in over 100 runs. Lifetime he batted .256 and hit 573 home runs, fifth on the all-time list behind Aaron, Ruth, Mays, and Frank Robinson.

7

Expansion

In 1961 the American League enlarged upon the eight-team structure that had prevailed in the major leagues since 1901 by expanding to ten teams. With the Dodgers and Giants, operating in California since 1958, having successfully established transcontinental baseball, the American League finally took the big leap and placed a new franchise in Los Angeles. Other virgin ground was broken in the St. Paul-Minneapolis area, the team being known as the Minnesota Twins.

Moving to Minnesota were the Washington Senators. The move had long been desired by Washington owner Calvin Griffith but had always been blocked by the league, which was reluctant to leave the nation's capital without major-league ball. With expansion, Griffith was finally given leave to depart, with a brand-new ball club being installed in Washington. The new clubs were stocked with players made available by the other eight teams.

The American League's move was made in response to the National League's announced plan to expand to a ten-team circuit in 1962, the new clubs being placed in New York and Houston.

The new, rather unwieldy ten-team structure necessitated a lengthening to a 162-game schedule, and this led into a controversy ignited by the most exciting season-long performance by a player in modern times—the Yankees' Roger Maris' pursuit of Babe Ruth's fabled record of 60 home runs in a season.

Maris had had a fine season in 1960, but still no one was prepared for what the twenty-six-year-old right fielder did in 1961. After a slow start—he didn't hit his first home run until the Yankees' eleventh game—he gradually built up a long-ball momentum that kept baseball fans enthralled throughout the summer. As Maris closed in on Ruth's record, the new, longer schedule became a factor. Baseball purists insisted that in order to tie or break Ruth's record, Maris had to do it in 154 games. Others maintained that a season was a season. Ford Frick, then commissioner, agreed with the purists, saying that if Maris broke the mark in the extra eight games, the feat would be so recorded in the record books.

As it turned out, Maris clouted number 60 in game 159 and the topper in game 163 (the Yanks played one tie that year) against Tracy Stallard of the Red Sox, at Yankee Stadium.

Maris' bombardment, spectacular as it was, was but one part of a fireworks display put on all summer by the Yankee lineup. The cannonading was fearsome, relentless, and consistent. Home run records fell by the fistful. The New Yorkers hit 240 seat-breakers, bettering by an astonishing 47 the American League record they had set the year before.

Mickey Mantle turned in a year of his own. Keeping pace with Maris until slowed by injuries in early September, Mantle powered 54 homers. The "M & M Boys" set a two-man record with 115 belts between them, beating out the old Ruth-Gehrig mark of 107, set in 1927. Behind Roger and Mickey came Bill Skowron with 28 homers, Yogi Berra 22, and Elston Howard and John Blanchard with 21 each.

Oddly enough, the Yankees did not lead the league in runs; the second-place Tigers outscored them, 841 to 827. Generally, it was a heavy-hitting season, if not for average, then for power. After Maris and Mantle, there were home run totals of 46 for Minnesota's Harmon Killebrew and Baltimore's Jim Gentile, 45 for Rocky Colavito and 41 for Norm Cash, both with Detroit, with Cash giving Detroit another batting title with an uncharacteristic .361 average (otherwise he never hit over .283 in a 17-year career).

Led by the Maris-Mantle combine and Whitey Ford's 25–4 record, the Yankees took a second straight pennant. It was the second of another five straight.

The Bronx Bombers cooled off to a mere 199 homers in 1962, with Maris dropping to 33 and Mantle to 30. The league's big bruiser was Minnesota's Killebrew, who whacked 48, taking the second of the six big-bang titles he would collect. Overall, the league hit 1,552 home runs in 1962, a record for the ten-team league.

In 1963 Ralph Houk's crew took the pennant by 10½ over the White Sox, Al Lopez once again watching it all happen from second place. The Yanks did it despite serious injuries to Maris, who played in only 90 games, and Mantle, who played in just 65 games. The talent-rich Yankees filled the gap by getting fine seasons out of Joe Pepitone and Tom Tresh. Ford was 24–7 and sophomore righty Jim Bouton 21–7.

The big noise in the league in 1963 came out of Minnesota, where 225 home runs were struck, second highest total in history. Killebrew launched 45, followed by outfielders Bob Allison and Jimmie Hall with 35 and 33 respectively, and catcher Earl Battey with 26. In spite of all the long-balling, none of these players drove in 100 runs for the third-place Twins, suggesting an all-or-nothing offense. The entire league seemed to have taken the same approach. The Twins' .255 batting average was high for the league, with .300 hitters as rare as square eggs. Boston's Carl Yastrzemski, then a twenty-three-year-old playing his third season, won the batting crown with a .321 mark.

In 1964 the Yankees again let go of a pennant-winning skipper. This time, however, it was to give him a promotion. After going 3 for 3 in pennants, Houk was elevated to general manager. His replacement was the genial Yogi Berra, at the end now of his Hall of Fame career.

The move proved a mistake, despite a late-season drive that gave the Yanks their second clutch of five straight. Everybody loved Yogi, but his Yankee buddies never seemed to take him seriously. A 22–6 September rush gave the Yankees the title by a one-game sliver over second-place Al Lopez and his scrappy White Sox. Al came close thanks to strong performances by left-handers Gary Peters (20–8) and Juan Pizarro (19–9), righty Joel Horlen, and a brilliant season from the forty-year-old knuckle-balling relief specialist Hoyt Wilhelm.

Minnesota finished seventh despite another barrage of 221 home runs, topped by Killebrew's 49. The year's golden arm belonged to Los Angeles' Dean Chance, a breezy young character who turned in a 20–9 record, a 1.65 ERA, and 11 shutouts, highest in the league since the William Taft administration, when Jack Coombs pitched 13 blankers for Connie Mack in 1910. The batting championship went to Minnesota rookie Tony Oliva, a twenty-three-year-old Cuban with a silver stroke, who batted .323.

After losing to the Cardinals in the 1964 World Series, the Yankees for the third time in five years got rid of a pennant-winning manager, dropping Berra. The man they hired was the man who had just beaten them, the Cardinals' Johnny Keane. Johnny was a good man, serious and highly respected, but he was being handed the captaincy of a baseball *Titanic*. Age, gravity, and the law of averages finally caught up to the Yankees, and what Ruth, Gehrig, DiMaggio, and Mantle had wrought for more than 40 years suddenly turned to wet bread and a long wandering in the wilderness. Mantle, Maris, and Howard surrendered their efficiency to injuries; other players had subpar years; the magic was leaving Whitey Ford's left arm; the farm system had stopped producing youthful over-achievers. Eleven years would slip by before another pennant rustled against the skies over Yankee Stadium.

In 1965 the Minnesota Twins stopped trotting, started running, finally got some good pitching, and won a pennant. They hit 71 fewer home runs than they did the year before, stole twice as many bases, got a 21–7 year from righty Jim ("Mudcat") Grant, 18–11 from lefty Jim Kaat, plus winning seasons from Jim Perry and relief pitchers Al Worthington and Johnny Klippstein, and rolled home seven games in front of Chicago and perennial bridesmaid Al Lopez. Surprisingly, the Twins did it despite an injury to their ace, Camilo Pascual, a right-hander as good as any in the league. Sidelined for six weeks, Pascual contributed a 9–3 record.

Though not as resonant as the year before, the Twins led the hitting-poor American League with a .254 team average, with Tony Oliva collecting another batting crown, this time with a .321 average. With Killebrew losing a third of the season to an elbow injury, the home run title went to Boston's twenty-year-old Tony Conigliaro, who hoisted 32 four-baggers, becoming the youngest player ever to lead in that most glamorous of hitting departments.

In 1966 the Baltimore Orioles, building carefully and patiently for years, finally had in place the team that would for years be one of the league's dominant and probably one of its greatest ever.

Behind young starting pitchers Jim Palmer, Dave McNally, Wally Bunker, and Steve Barber, who were picked up now and then by a couple of relief artists named Eddie Fisher and Stu Miller, the Orioles followed a steady and inexorable path to the 1966 pennant, finishing nine games ahead of the defending champs, Minnesota. The Orioles had massive John ("Boog") Powell at first base and Dave Johnson at second, both products of the farm system (as were most of the starting pitchers). At short was Luis Aparicio, obtained from the White Sox several years earlier, and at third Brooks Robinson, now a full-fledged star. Paul Blair and Russ Snyder were in the outfield with the man who had been the final piece needed to complete the Oriole picture.

A long-time star in the National League with Cincinnati, Frank Robinson had been traded to the Orioles for pitcher Milt Pappas even-up. The curious rationale given by the Reds for the deal (Pappas was a good pitcher, but not good enough to go even-up for Robinson) was that the thirty-year-old Robinson was an "old thirty." The assessment rankled the proud Robinson. Sixteen years later, when he was being inducted into the Hall of Fame in 1982, he still remembered. "People ask what drives Frank Robinson," he said in accepting induction at Cooperstown. "One thing was when I was traded by the Reds. They said I was 'an old thirty.' That was the turning point."

Robinson, an inspired and inspirational ballplayer and a man with a natural flair for leadership, was driven all season to prove that the charge of premature dotage was ill advised. He swept the Triple Crown with a .316 batting average, 49 home runs, and 122 runs batted in. His Most Valuable Player Award matched the one he had won with the Reds in 1961, making him the only man ever to take the honor in both leagues.

The Orioles sank to sixth place in 1967, due to an arm injury to young Palmer that nearly ended his career, and a sharp drop in games won by Bunker, Barber, and McNally. What happened at the top of the league, however, was one of the most thrilling pennant chases in history.

Four teams were in the hunt until the season's final week—Boston, Chicago, Detroit, and Minnesota. Chicago, with a team batting average of .225, hung on through the pitching of Joel Horlen, Gary Peters, Tommy John, bullpen operatives Hoyt Wilhelm, Bob Locker, and Don McMahon, and a spirited run-and-steal attack. Minnesota followed the rollicking bats of Killebrew, Oliva, and young second baseman Rod Carew to the bitter end. Detroit had Al Kaline, Bill Freehan, Norm Cash, and Willie Horton, and pitchers Earl Wilson (22–11), Denny McLain, Joe Sparma,

and Mickey Lolich. But the Tigers and Twins came up a game short at the end because the Boston Red Sox had two irresistible forces— Carl Yastrzemski and a miracle that has gone down in Boston baseball lore as "the Impossible Dream."

Rising from the ashes of a ninth-place finish in 1966, the Red Sox, driven and tongue-lashed by rookie skipper Dick Williams, won their first flag in 21 years on the last day of the season, thanks to Yastrzemski's heroic 4 for 4 in the finale against the Twins and some gutsy pitching by 22-game winner Jim Lonborg.

"Carl Yastrzemski in 1967 was the greatest player I've ever seen," Manager Dick Williams said. Signed for a $100,000 bonus, Yaz joined the Red Sox in 1961, a twenty-one-year-old left fielder heralded as the successor to Ted Williams. An incomparable fielder with a deadly arm, it took the sometimes moody youngster several years to hit his stride. In 1967, along with first baseman George Scott, shortstop Rico Petrocelli, and rookie outfielder Reggie Smith, Yaz helped weave the Impossible Dream with a Triple Crown performance, hitting .326, belting 44 home runs (tied by Killebrew), and driving in 121 runs.

The Sox did it despite the loss in August of their young home run-hitting outfielder Tony Conigliaro, who was struck in the face by a Jack Hamilton fast ball. The injury sidelined Conigliaro for the rest of the year and spelled the beginning of the end of what had promised to be an exciting career.

For several years batting averages had been plummeting and in 1968 the nadir was reached, particularly in the American League, which posted the lowest batting average in its history, .230. A record for most shutouts for a ten-club league was also set, 154. Carl Yastrzemski won the batting crown with a .301 average, lowest in big-league history for a titlist.

It is remembered as "the Year of the Pitcher," and the wretched batting averages were reflected in earned-run averages. Cleveland's Luis Tiant was top dog with a 21–9 record and 1.60 ERA, followed by teammate Sam McDowell, who had a 1.81 ERA. McDowell, called "Sudden Sam," was one of the game's genuine strikeout artists. The tall left-hander could fire as hard as anybody, leading in whiffs five times, with a high of 325 in 1965. Other handsome earned-run averages in 1968 were Dave McNally's 1.95, Dennis McLain's 1.96, and Tommy John's 1.98.

The story in 1968 was McLain. The twenty-four-year-old Detroit right-hander hurled his club to the pennant with an astounding 31–6 record, the league's first 30-timer since Grove won 31 in 1931. McLain was not a totally unknown quantity, having won 20 in 1966; even so, if anyone would have predicted who the next 30-game winner might be, the consensus would probably have been McDowell because of the missile he threw.

McLain, one of the game's all-time blithe spirits, was a strutting rooster on the mound, brash and confident, with a personality as noticeable as a sunrise. He was quick, with a sharp breaking ball. He was also credited by one of his catchers as having had instincts on the mound so uncanny as to almost amount to a sixth sense. Denny (he was Lou Boudreau's son-in-law) seemed at times able to read the minds of opposing batters.

Behind McLain was Mickey Lolich, a durable lefty with a sinking fast ball, who was 17–9. Detroit's offense in the Year of the Pitcher was generated by Willie Horton with 36 homers and by Norm Cash and Bill Freehan, who must have been watching each other closely all season, for each banged 25 homers and batted .263, noteworthy numbers that year.

There was another franchise shift before the 1968 season opened. The Kansas City Athletics, already once removed from their ancestral home in Philadelphia, now moved even farther away from the ghost of Connie Mack and settled in Oakland, where soon they would begin making much noise and history. Already on the Oakland squad was a sharp young right-hander named Jim ("Catfish") Hunter who caught the eye of the baseball world with a perfect game against the Twins on May 8, the league's first perfecto since Chicago's Charley Robertson did it in 1922. Also playing for Oakland in 1968 was a sparkling young shortstop named Bert Campaneris, a quiet outfielder named Joe Rudi, and a chesty one with a power swing named Reggie Jackson. This is what is known as a nucleus. Jackson gave American League fans a good look at two of his specialties in his first full season: 29 home runs and 171 strikeouts. Pitching one inning for Oakland that year was a tall, twenty-one-year-old right-hander named Rollie Fingers. Rollie had a rough inning, allowing four hits and a walk and slept that winter on a major-league ERA of 36.00. But he would do better.

Both leagues ballooned to twelve teams in 1969, the American enrolling outposts in Seattle and a fresh entry for Kansas City. In order to prevent a pile of twelve teams from tottering, the league was split in half—the eastern division for New York, Boston, Baltimore, Detroit, Washington, and Cleveland; a western division for Oakland, Minnesota, California (as the Los Angeles club had rechristened itself), Chicago, Seattle, and Kansas City. From out of this was invented two champions and a best three-out-of-five championship series to crown a pennant winner.

Baltimore ran away with the first eastern division title in 1969, winning 109 games for skipper Earl Weaver and leaving defending champ Detroit choking in the dust of a 19-game deficit. Weaver's club may have been the league's best since the 1927 Yankees. With steady bats and sparkling gloves everywhere to be found, the O's made a shambles of the race. Boog Powell popped 37 home runs, Frank Robinson 32, Paul Blair 26, and Brooks Robinson 23. Robinson had playing alongside him now shortstop Mark Belanger, a glove as good as Aparicio's. The left side of the Orioles was as good as hermitically sealed. With other magic gloves belonging to Dave Johnson at second and Blair in center, all the Oriole pitchers had to do was let the batter hit the ball.

The Oriole pitchers, though, were their own men. Lefty Mike Cuellar, a National League retread, won 23; Dave McNally won 20, and Jim Palmer 16. This Big Three became the most proficient mound trio to work for the same employer since the gaudy days of Lemon, Wynn, and Garcia in Cleveland.

Winning in the West was Minnesota, once again led by the thunder of Harmon Killebrew's 49 home runs and 140 runs batted in. With the mound having been lowered and the strike zone contracted by a league not wanting a repetition of 1968's feeble hitting, some respectable batting averages were again turned in. The league's most respectable was registered by Minnesota's twenty-three-year-old Rod Carew, who led with a .332 mark, beginning what would be for him a most pleasing habit.

Oakland's Reggie Jackson became a bona fide big ripper in 1969, belting 47 home runs, while Washington's walking mountain, Frank Howard, delivered 48 all-the-way jobs. Detroit's Denny McLain followed up his monumental season with a fine 24–9 record. It marked the tail of Denny's comet; the following year a bad arm and some off-the-field shenanigans took the sizzle out of what looked like a Hall of Fame career.

The American League's first championship series was a shutout for Baltimore—they rolled over Minnesota in three straight.

The 1970 races were carbon copies of the year before, and so was the championship series. The Orioles won 108 games for Earl Weaver and then rolled over Minnesota in three straight again, led by the irresistible arms of Cuellar (24–8), McNally (24–9), and Palmer (20–10). The Twins had a 24-gamer in righty Jim Perry and the usual resonance from Killebrew, who launched 41 home runs, second to Frank Howard's 44, and a .325 season from the splendid Tony Oliva. The Twins lost Rod Carew for most of the season, a knee injury putting Rodney on the shelf after 51 games and a .366 batting average.

The season was a spoiled pudding for Dennis McLain. By September the Golden Boy had tarnish all over him. Commissioner Bowie Kuhn suspended the Detroit ace in February for having become involved with gamblers a few years before. Supposedly, Denny had helped bankroll a bookmaking operation, a corker of a sideline for any professional athlete. On July 1 he was reinstated, but by then the hum was gone from his fast ball. He got another week's suspension later on for dumping buckets of ice water on a couple of sports writers, no doubt every ballplayer's fantasy at one time or another, but not within the code of accepted behavior. On September 9 Kuhn hunkered him down for the rest of the season for carrying a gun. Why Denny was thusly fortifying himself is not certain. It could have been to protect himself against vengeful sports writers or perhaps against the assaults of American League hitters—he ended with a 3–5 record and an inflated ERA. At the end of the season the Tigers unloaded him on Washington, where he soon took the fast lane to oblivion.

Roger Maris. Roger came to the big leagues with Cleveland in 1957, was traded to Kansas City the next year and two years later to New York. In 1960 he hit 39 home runs and was voted MVP. A year later he hit his 61 homers, drove in 142 runs, and was again voted MVP. He finished up with the Cardinals in 1968. Maris has a career batting average of .260 and 275 home runs.

Mickey Mantle.

Bill Skowron, the Yankees' muscular first baseman from 1954 to 1962, after which he played for four more teams, retiring in 1967. Five times a .300 hitter, Skowron's lifetime average is .282.

Right-hander Ralph Terry, a 23-game winner for the Yankees in 1962. Pitching for four teams from 1956 to 1967, Ralph had his top years with the Yankees in the early 1960s. Lifetime he was 107–99.

First baseman Jim Gentile played from 1957 to 1966 with five different clubs. His big year was 1961 with Baltimore, when he hit 46 home runs and had 141 runs batted in. Lifetime he batted .260.

Southpaw Hank Aguirre was the ERA leader in 1962 with 2.21 and a 16–8 record. Hank pitched from 1955 to 1970, mostly with Detroit. Lifetime record: 75–72.

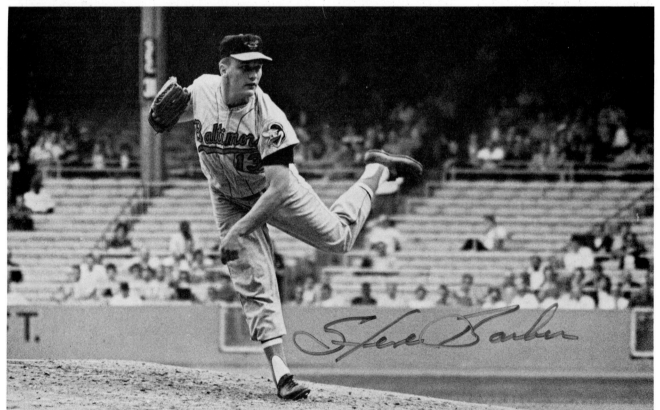

Between 1960 and 1974 Steve Barber pitched for seven teams, but he never recaptured the magic he had in his early years with Baltimore. He won 18 in 1961 and was 20–13 in 1963. Lifetime he was 121–106.

Norm Cash came to the bigs with the White Sox in 1958, was traded to the Tigers two years later, and there he stayed until 1974. In 1961 Norm belted 41 home runs and led the league with a .361 batting average. Overall he hit 377 homers and batted .271.

Joel Horlen, fine White Sox right-hander from 1961 to 1971. In 1967 he led in ERA with 2.06 and had a 19–7 record. Lifetime he was 116–117.

The infield of the 1963–1964 Yankee pennant winners. Left to right: third baseman Clete Boyer, shortstop Tony Kubek, second baseman Bobby Richardson, first baseman Joe Pepitone.

Right-hander Camilo Pascual came to the majors with Washington in 1954 and enjoyed his best years after the team moved to Minnesota, winning 20 in 1962 and 21 in 1963. A three-time leader in strikeouts, Pascual pitched until 1971. Considered by many as one of the best pitchers of his day, his lifetime record stands at 174–170.

Gary Peters, one of the league's better left-handers during his career, which ran from 1959 through 1972, all but the last three years spent with the White Sox. He led in ERA in 1963 and 1966 and was a 20-game winner in 1964. Finishing up with the Red Sox, his career record read 124–103.

Right-hander Milt Pappas pitched for Baltimore from 1957 through 1965, when he was traded to Cincinnati for Frank Robinson. He pitched in the National League until 1973. Although never winning more than 17 games in a season, he ended up with a 209–164 record.

Dick Radatz, right-handed Red Sox relief pitcher in the early 1960s who was known as "the Monster." Almost unhittable his first three seasons, he tapered off after 1964. Pitching for four other clubs until retiring in 1969, his lifetime record is 52–43.

Cleveland third baseman Max Alvis. Max played from 1962 to 1970 and batted .247.

Colorful, unpredictable southpaw Bo Belinsky, who bounced around with five clubs between 1962 and 1970, winning 28 and losing 51. He no-hit Baltimore in 1962 while pitching for the Angels.

Second baseman Jerry Lumpe came up with the Yankees in 1956 but spent most of his career with Kansas City and Detroit, retiring in 1967 with a lifetime average of .268.

Bob Allison, power hitter with the Washington Senators—Minnesota Twins from 1958 to 1970. His big year was 1963, when he hit 35 homers. Lifetime batting average: .255.

Harmon Killebrew about to give it his all.

Minnesota skipper Sam Mele getting an enthusiastic heave-ho from umpire Bill Valentine in July 1965. Earl Battey is the catcher.

Earl Battey, strong-hitting catcher with the White Sox and Twins from 1955 to 1967. Earl batted .270 lifetime.

Jim Perry, older of the two pitching Perrys. Jim pitched from 1959 through 1975, mostly with Cleveland and Minnesota. He was a 20-game winner in 1969 and 1970. Lifetime record: 215–174.

Outfielder Jimmie Hall hit 33 homers in his rookie year for the Twins, 1963. He played for Minnesota until 1966, then for five other teams before retiring in 1970 with a .254 career average.

Tony Oliva, Minnesota's sweet-swinging three-time batting champ. Tony also led in hits five times and doubles four times. His career average is .304.

Jim ("Mudcat") Grant pitched for seven teams from 1958 through 1971. His best year was 1965, when he was 21–7 for Minnesota. Lifetime he was 145–119.

First baseman John ("Boog") Powell, shown here with Rochester of the International League in 1961. Boog played in the big leagues from 1961 to 1977, all but three of those years with the Orioles. In 1969 he hit 37 home runs and drove in 121 runs. Lifetime he hit 339 homers and batted .266.

Brooks Robinson, Baltimore's model for third basemen. He played for Baltimore for 23 years, 1955 through 1977, collecting 2,848 hits and batting .267. In 1964 he batted .317, led in RBIs with 118, and was the league's Most Valuable Player. His 2,870 games at third base is by far the all-time record.

Frank Robinson. Lifetime statistics: 2,943 hits, 586 home runs, .294 batting average.

Right-hander Wally Bunker. He had a fine 19–5 rookie season for Baltimore in 1964, but never came close to equaling it. He pitched until 1971, finishing up with Kansas City. Lifetime record: 60–52.

Jim Palmer in 1965, his rookie year with Baltimore.

266

Dave Johnson, Baltimore second baseman from 1965 to 1972, when he was
traded to the National League. He retired in 1978 with a batting average of
.261.

Carl Yastrzemski.

Right-hander Earl Wilson. He came up with the Red Sox in 1959 and was traded to Detroit in 1966. A year later he had his best season, 22–11. He retired in 1970 with a 121–109 record.

Jim Lonborg, a 22-game winner for the pennant-winning Red Sox in 1967. He pitched for three teams from 1965 to 1979, winning 157 and losing 137.

Reggie Smith in 1967, his first full year with the Red Sox, for whom he played until he was traded to the Cardinals in 1974.

Sam McDowell. "Sudden Sam," who could throw as hard as anybody, pitched for Cleveland from 1961 through 1971, when he was traded to the Giants. He pitched until 1975, retiring with a 141–134 record. His biggest year was 1970, when he was 20–12. Sam led in strikeouts five times, topping himself with 325 in 1965.

Mel Stottlemyre, smooth-pitching Yankee ace from 1964 through 1974. Three times a 20-game winner, he was 164–139 lifetime.

Dean Chance, major-league pitcher from 1961 to 1971. He was 20–9 with the Angels in 1964 and 20–14 with the Twins in 1967. Lifetime he was 128–115.

Mickey Lolich, the steady, durable left-hander of the Detroit Tigers from 1963 through 1976, when he was traded to the New York Mets. Mickey won 25 in 1971, 22 the next year. He retired in 1979 with a 217–191 record.

Denny McLain, 31–6 in 1968, 24–9 in 1969. Lifetime: 131–91.

Detroit has just scored in the bottom of the ninth inning against Oakland on September 14, 1968, giving Denny McLain his thirtieth victory of the season. Leaping out of the dugout is McLain (capless) along with Al Kaline.

Willie Horton, power-hitting outfielder for Detroit and five other clubs from 1963 to 1980. Willie had 36 home runs in 1968, 325 over his career, during which he batted .273.

Bill Freehan, one of the great catchers in Detroit history. He played for the Tigers from 1961 through 1976, batting .262.

There are over 75,000 fans packed into Yankee Stadium for this July 1961 game.

Outfielder Frank Howard put baseballs into orbit from 1958 to 1973. Coming up with the Dodgers, he was traded to Washington in 1965. He led with 44 homers in 1968 and 44 again in 1970. In 1969 he hit 48, losing the title by one to Killebrew. Lifetime he hit 382 four-baggers and batted .273

Jim Fregosi, fine shortstop for the Angels from 1961 through 1971, when he was traded to the Mets for Nolan Ryan. Jim played until 1978, batting .265 for his career.

Dave Boswell pitched for the Twins from 1964 to 1970, with one big year in 1969, when he was 20–12. Lifetime he was 68–56.

Jim Northrup, Tiger outfielder from 1964 to 1974. He retired in 1975 after a year with Baltimore. Lifetime batting average: .267.

Luis Tiant in 1964, his rookie year with Cleveland.

Comiskey Park, Chicago, later rechristened White Sox Park, home of the White Sox since 1910.

Earl Weaver, manager of the Baltimore Orioles, in 1969, his first full year as skipper.

Memorial Stadium, Baltimore, home of the Baltimore Orioles.

Mike Cuellar was traded to Baltimore from Houston in 1969 and went on to four 20-game seasons for the Orioles before retiring in 1977. Lifetime record: 185–130.

Dave McNally, Baltimore's stellar southpaw from 1962 through 1974. He won 20 or more four straight seasons, 1968–1971. He retired with Montreal in 1975 with a lifetime record of 184–119.

Paul Blair, Baltimore's superb center fielder from 1964 through 1976. He retired with the Yankees in 1980 with a lifetime batting average of .250.

Baltimore's Mark Belanger, after Aparicio the league's premier glove at shortstop.

At bat: Reggie Jackson of the Oakland Athletics. That ball looks like it's going for a ride.

Jim ("Catfish") Hunter. Lifetime record: 224–166.

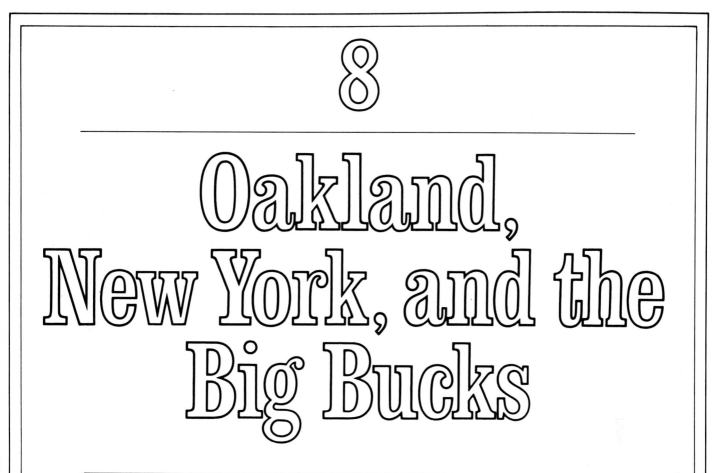

8

Oakland, New York, and the Big Bucks

The records of the top four on the Baltimore pitching staff in 1971 read as follows: Dave McNally 21–5, Pat Dobson 20–8, Mike Cuellar 20–9, Jim Palmer 20–9. Four 20-game winners tied the major-league record set by the Chicago White Sox staff in 1920. Behind these four smoothly cruising vessels, Earl Weaver's boys easily took a third straight division title and then a third straight pennant, bumping the Oakland A's in three straight, giving the Orioles a 9–0 record for championship series outings.

For Oakland, it was their first division title, and by now most of their stars had arrived. The pitching was led by a twenty-one-year-old lefty with a high kick and a whistling fast ball, Vida Blue. Virtually unbeatable in the first half, he finished the season with a 24–8 record, 301 strikeouts, and a 1.82 ERA. Catfish Hunter launched the first of five 20-game-winning seasons with a 21–11 record. Rollie Fingers had by now established himself as a bullpen ace. Reggie Jackson hit 32 boomers, second by one to Chicago's Bill Melton.

The batting title went for the third time to Minnesota's Tony Oliva, who hit .337. But Tony played in just 126 games, missing the last six weeks after hurting his knee diving for a line drive. The injury was to curtail Tony's effectiveness, and although he continued to play until 1976, it was as a designated hitter and never again did he hit .300.

After the 1971 season, Oakland obtained Chicago Cubs left-hander Ken Holtzman in a trade for outfielder Rick Monday. This gave the club all the pitching they needed and made them deadly in a short series, which they proved after taking western division titles in 1972, 1973, and 1974 by winning the championship series and then World Series each year.

It was this formidable pitching staff, dominated by Holtzman, Hunter, Blue and Fingers, that gave the Oakland A's their aura of greatness. Despite three successive world championships, the club was not the measure of the recent Baltimore contingents or of earlier Yankee teams. Through their three triumphant years, they had only one .300 hitter, Joe Rudi's .305 in 1972. Along with Joe, a superb left fielder, the other genuine stars of the team were shortstop Bert Campaneris and Reggie Jackson. Third baseman Sal Bando was a solid performer, providing stability, leadership, and clutch hitting. Gene Tenace, dividing his time behind the plate and at first base, lent some power. Dick Green was a light-hitting second baseman with a magic glove.

A team of personalities, enlivened occasionally by clubhouse punch-outs among themselves, they were united by two things: a spirited zest to win, and their dislike for owner Charles O. Finley, who goaded them, criticized them, and frequently outraged them. The "O" in Finley's name stood for Oscar, but Charlie made it plain it also stood for "Owner." He changed managers on an almost yearly basis, badgered the league into adopting the designated hitter rule in 1973, advocated night ball in the World Series, and urged the use of an orange baseball. In 1972 he offered a cash bonus to any of his players who grew a mustache and the resulting sprouts made the A's the most colorful band of athletes in the country.

In 1972 the Orioles slipped to third place in the East as the Tigers under Billy Martin won the division behind Mickey Lolich's 22 wins and 19 by righty Joe Coleman, who had been obtained from Washington in the Mc-Lain deal. The Tigers, however, lost to Oakland in a tightly played championship series, three games to two.

The year saw a spectacular MVP perform-

ance by Chicago's Richie Allen, obtained in a deal with the Dodgers for Tommy John. Allen kayoed American League pitching for a .308 batting average, 37 home runs, and 113 runs batted in, the latter two numbers the best in the league. Richie was rewarded for this noble display with what was then a record contract for 1973—$250,000. Another National League transplant, Gaylord Perry, obtained by Cleveland from San Francisco in a swap for Sam McDowell, was the league's top pitcher with a 24–16 record.

There was also another franchise shift, the second in two years (in 1970 Seattle had dropped out and Milwaukee come in). For the second time, Washington lost its club, the team being hauled west and set down in Arlington, Texas, midway between Dallas and Fort Worth and named the Texas Rangers. For the first time the nation's capital was without big-league ball. ("We have been without big-league ball for decades," observed a long-suffering Washington fan morosely.)

In 1973 Baltimore climbed back to the top in the East, again behind the sturdy arms of Palmer, Cuellar, and McNally, only to bow in five to Oakland. The A's had the league's top home run and RBI man in Reggie Jackson, along with 20-game seasons from Hunter, Blue, and Holtzman, and incomparable relief work from Fingers (the most valuable man on those championship teams, according to teammate Tenace. Owner Finley thought Campaneris was the club's most valuable asset. Reggie Jackson probably didn't agree with either).

Minnesota's Carew, having won the batting crown in 1972, took another, his third, in 1973, with a .350 average. This was the year that Nolan Ryan, acquired by the California Angels from the New York Mets the year before in one of the game's most memorable steal-deals, fanned his record 383 batters. The fireballer did it in storybook fashion, too. Going into his final start of the year on September 28 against the Twins needing 15 strikeouts to equal Sandy Koufax's major-league record, Ryan got 16, though needing an 11-inning game to get the record breaker. (Attention trivia buffs: the name of strikeout victim number 383 was Rich Reese.)

It was a tasty season for Ryan. In addition to his strikeout record and his 21 wins, the twenty-six-year-old burner also pitched two no-hitters.

In 1974 Baltimore repeated in the East, winning by two games over a rejuvenated New York Yankee club now principally owned by a Cleveland shipbuilder named George Steinbrenner, who solemnly promised New York fans he would soon produce a winner for them. The O's did it by winning 28 of their last 34 games, a fairly typical late-season surge by this team, which had a genius for keeping its pitchers fresh throughout the long season. Weaver had another 20-game winner in Cuellar, Mike winning 22 to lead the staff. Twenty-game winners seemed to grow out of the Baltimore mound like weeds in an empty lot.

Detroit's graceful veteran Al Kaline retired that October after collecting his three thousandth hit, doing it playing the entire season as a designated hitter, a fact that made some record-book purists snort. Minnesota's Carew, tapping base hits every which way, took another batting crown, with a .364 average that was built upon 218 hits, 180 of them singles. Ryan won 22 games for his last-place California club, whiffed 367 batters, and delivered a third no-hitter.

Oakland's fourth straight division title in 1974 was again fashioned by the arms of Hunter, Blue, Holtzman, and the tireless Fingers. Hunter, the ace of aces on this staff, was 25–12. The A's again topped the O's in the championship series, three games to one, limiting the Orioles to just one run over the last 27 innings. A year later, much to the chagrin of Oakland fans, Hunter was wearing a Yankee uniform.

Hunter's contract had specified certain payments be made; when Finley did not make the payments—either through oversight or outright refusal—Hunter took the matter to arbitration and was declared a free agent by virtue of breach of contract. Catfish then put his services on the open market, and for the first time ballplayers realized just how much the clubs were willing to pay for their services. With almost every big-league club in the bidding, Hunter finally signed a five-year contract with the Yankees for a package estimated to be worth upwards of $3 million. The determined Yankee owner who refused to be outbid for Hunter was George Steinbrenner, soon to become the most conspicuous, outrageous, fascinating, and successful club owner in baseball.

It was in 1975 that the American League finally stole a march in racial progress on the National by signing the major leagues' first black manager. The team was Cleveland and the man was Frank Robinson, now in the sputtering final days of his great career. Robinson's distinction assured him of another—he would also be the first black manager ever to be fired (he was canned two years later).

Nolan Ryan pitched a fourth no-hitter, matching another Koufax record, and Rod Carew took his fifth batting crown and fourth in a row, with a .359 mark. The Minnesota second baseman was becoming the most prolific winner of batting titles since Cobb.

Catfish Hunter performed as expected for the Yankees, winning 23; Baltimore had 20-game winners in Jim Palmer and Mike Torrez; but the surprise club in the eastern division was the Red Sox. Thanks to some steady pitching by veterans Rick Wise, Luis Tiant, and left-hander Bill Lee, the Sox were able to stay in it all the way, beating out Baltimore by 4½. To a batting attack that already included Carl Yastrzemski, Dwight Evans, Carlton Fisk, and Cecil Cooper, the Red Sox added a pair of hard-hitting rookie outfielders—Jim Rice and Fred Lynn. Rice batted .309, hit 22 home runs, and drove in 102 runs; Lynn batted .331 with 21 homers and 105 runs batted in. Lynn, a gifted center fielder, achieved the unprecedented distinction of winning both Rookie-of-the-Year and Most Valuable Player honors.

In the West, Oakland surprised a lot of people by winning 98 games and the division title despite the loss of Hunter. They also surprised a lot of people by falling in three straight to the Red Sox in the championship series.

In 1975 two pitchers played the season without signing contracts. They were Andy Messersmith of the Los Angeles Dodgers and Dave McNally, formerly of the Orioles, now with the Montreal Expos. The men were putting to the test their belief that a team "owned" a player for the length of his contract plus one year—the "option year"—and no longer. The teams claimed that the option year was self-renewing under the conditions of the reserve clause. On December 24, 1975, arbitrator Peter Seitz ruled in favor of the players. (McNally, lending his name to the case, retired; Messersmith was signed to a lucrative contract by the Atlanta Braves.) Players could now play out their option year and then be free to sell their services to the highest bidder. The era of free agency and sumptuous contracts was about to begin.

In order to prevent total chaos, an agreement was reached between players and owners in the spring of 1976 stating that any player who wished could become a free agent after six years in the major leagues. As a transition measure, anyone playing without a signed contract in 1976 would become a free agent after that season, the same going for 1977.

It was not just the free agents who were going to make all the money. In order to hold on to their stars, the clubs were going to have to offer contracts commensurate with the market value.

Alarmed by the thought of losing his star players to free agency without any compensa-tion, and unwilling to meet their anticipated salary demands, Oakland owner Charles Finley began a hasty dismantling of his fine team. He traded Reggie Jackson and Ken Holtzman to Baltimore for Don Baylor and Mike Torrez. In mid-June he tried to sell Joe Rudi and Rollie Fingers to the Red Sox and Vida Blue to the Yankees, each transaction straight cash amounting to around a million dollars for each player. Commissioner Kuhn stepped in, however, voiding the deals on the grounds that they "were not in the best interests of baseball." The feisty Finley accused Kuhn of abuse of power and headed for the courts (the judge eventually ruled for Kuhn).

Many baseball fans found the wrangling, the threatened litigation, and all the talk of millions of dollars distasteful as well as a little bit confusing. But much of this was dissipated by the timely appearance on the scene in 1976 of a youngster with a talent that was exceptional and an approach to his game that was both uninhibited and refreshing. His name was Mark Fidrych, he was a right-handed pitcher for the Tigers, and he was colorful, exciting, and a winner. Fidrych was 19–9, led in ERA and complete games, talked to the ball, shook hands with his infielders after good plays, cavorted with the pure joy and unrestrained enthusiasm of a Little Leaguer, and spent the summer pitching before packed houses.

After 12 years of empty Octobers, the Yankees returned to the top in 1976, managed now by their former second baseman Billy Martin. Thanks to the acquisition of Hunter and some judicious dealing in the flesh markets that had brought them pitchers Ed Figueroa and Sparky Lyle, first baseman Chris Chambliss, second baseman Willie Randolph, third baseman Graig Nettles, and outfielders Lou Piniella and Mickey Rivers, in addition to farm system product Thurman Munson behind the plate, the Yankees had put together another strong, dominant team.

The New Yorkers outran Earl Weaver's

Orioles by 10½ lengths, despite 20-game seasons by perennial 20-game winner Jim Palmer and Wayne Garland, giving the O's seventeen 20-game winners in nine years.

In the West the Kansas City Royals finally broke Oakland's grip on the high rung, finishing 2½ ahead of the A's. Oakland skipper Chuck Tanner poured some high octane into his boys, turned them loose, and watched them set a new league record with 341 stolen bases. Outfielder Billy North was the top rabbit with 75 steals, followed by Campaneris with 54, Don Baylor 52, Claudell Washington with 37, and Phil Garner with 35. Kansas City, however, had a bright young star in twenty-three-year-old third baseman George Brett, who led the league in batting with .333, beating out teammate Hal McRae by one point and Rod Carew by two.

The Yankees beat Kansas City in the championship series in five games, winning it on a dramatic bottom-of-the-ninth home run by Chris Chambliss, who batted .524 in the five games.

The free agents hit the market that November, and George Steinbrenner was waiting with a checkbook spread wide open from the Battery to the Bronx. Intent on building another Yankee dynasty, he landed the cream of the free agents: Baltimore's Reggie Jackson and Cincinnati's ace lefty Don Gullett. Reggie, baseball's premier personality and one of its genuine power men, received around $3 million and Gullett about a million less.

"You're not going to believe the bullshit," said an amused Ken Holtzman (now with the Yankees) of his former Oakland teammate as he awaited Reggie's arrival in New York. Jackson, who was New York in the same sense that Ruth had been, came bustling into spring training predicting he'd have a candy bar named after him (he eventually did), proclaiming an IQ that matched his slugging might, alienating team leader Thurman Munson, and irritating Billy Martin to the point where they nearly had a swing-out in the dug-out in front of a national television audience.

But Reggie could back it up, the way oversized personalities like Babe Ruth and Dizzy Dean had been able to. He slammed 32 home runs and drove in 110, joining Nettles, Munson, Rivers, Piniella, and Chambliss in fashioning an old-fashioned Yankee attack that drove the club to another division title, 2½ games over Baltimore and Boston. Hampered by injuries that would soon abort his career, Gullett was 14–4, while Hunter was just 9–9, also in an injury-racked season. The staff was picked up, however, by a skinny, hard-firing left-hander out of the farm system named Ron Guidry, a young man whose personality was as modest as his pitching was spectacular. In his first full season, Guidry was 16–7 with a 2.82 ERA.

The Red Sox unloaded 213 home runs, fourth highest total in American League history, led by Jim Rice's league-leading 39, followed by George Scott (33), Butch Hobson (30), Carl Yastrzemski (28), and Carlton Fisk (26). But the traditional Red Sox bugaboo, lack of quality pitching, held them back, relief pitcher Bill Campbell's 13 wins topping the staff.

While Kansas City repeated in the West, easily outdistancing Texas, the most interesting individual performance in baseball in 1977 was turned in by Minnesota's Rod Carew. After flirting with .400 throughout most of the summer, Carew checked in at season's end with a .388 average and 239 hits, taking a sixth batting crown.

It was a fourteen-team league now, expansion having reached out to station teams in Toronto and, once again, Seattle. True to the tradition of expansion teams, Toronto bottomed out the division in the East with 107 losses, while Seattle managed a moral victory by escaping the cellar by a half game, losing 98 games but winning one more than the once-powerful Oakland A's. Stripped by free agency, the A's had gone from supremacy to mediocrity in two years.

Perhaps the league's biggest loser in 1977 was fifth-place California. The Angels had plunged deeply and expensively into the free agent market, picking up Oakland's Joe Rudi and Don Baylor and Baltimore's Bobby Grich, three top talents. Injuries, however, held Rudi to just 64 games and Grich to 52, while Baylor labored through a subpar .251 season. Nolan Ryan kept whistling his fast ball without diminishment, posting a 19–16 record for a losing team and striking out 341 in 299 innings. Ryan's control problems continued to keep him from true greatness. Almost unhittable—he had an average yield of less than six hits per nine innings—he ended up walking 204 men.

The Yankees and the Royals again went to five games and again New York snatched the prize away from Kansas City in the ninth inning of the last game with a three-run rally.

It looked like the Red Sox all the way in the eastern division in 1978. For once, the two-fisted Bosox slugging attack was backed by some strong pitching. Dennis Eckersley, obtained in a trade with Cleveland, was 20–8, while free agent acquisition Mike Torrez was 16–13, and bullpen ace Bob Stanley was 15–2. Heading Boston's list of heavyweights was Jim Rice with one of the most sustained hitting attacks seen in years. Rice led with 46 homers, 15 triples, 213 hits, 139 runs batted in, .600 slugging average, and 406 total bases, this latter figure the league's best since Joe DiMaggio's 418 in 1937.

The Yankees, meanwhile, were undergoing a case of turmoil that was to become familiar with them. The leading roles in the New York drama were played by Steinbrenner, Martin, and Jackson, three Grand Canyon-sized egos trying to coexist under the same roof. Billy and Reggie were snarling at each other all year, while Steinbrenner was putting his thumbs to Martin for the team's poor showing. Unable to handle Jackson, whom he suspended for five games in July for ignoring a sign, threatened constantly with dismissal by Steinbrenner, Martin finally cracked in late July. It was a memorable wisecrack that did Billy in. Referring to his two chief tormentors, he said, "One is a confirmed liar" (meaning Reggie), "and the other is a convicted liar." This latter reference to some legal high jinks Steinbrenner had been caught up in with the government a few years before led directly to Martin's resignation under pressure.

When Bob Lemon took over the club on July 24, the Yankees were 10½ games behind a smoothly sailing Red Sox ship of state. But then the Yankees started winning and winning. Propelled by Jackson's big bat and a year from Guidry that was breathtaking, the New Yorkers stormed on, winning 48 of their last 68 to end in a tie with the Red Sox. The big man was Guidry, turning in a 25–3 season for an .893 winning percentage. His 1.74 ERA and nine shutouts topped the league. Figueroa had a 20–9 season, while free agent pickup Rich Gossage began paying dividends on a huge contract with 10 wins and 27 saves, teaming with Sparky Lyle to give the club an airtight bullpen.

Ending with identical 99–63 records, the Yankees and Red Sox played a one-game tie breaker in Fenway Park to determine the eastern division winner. The New Yorkers won it, 5–4, the big blow being a three-run homer by shortstop Bucky Dent. The Yankees' fifth run, the winning run, was scored on a homer by Jackson, Reggie having by now perfected his knack for these kinds of heroics.

With Kansas City taking a third straight title in the West, it was another New York–Kansas City match-up in the championship series. For the third year in a row, the Yankees frustrated the Royals, putting them away in four games this time, winning game three despite three home runs struck by George Brett.

There was triumph and tragedy in the league that year. California's large-sized free agent buy, twenty-seven-year-old sharp-hitting outfielder Lyman Bostock, formerly of the Twins, was shot and killed in Gary, Indiana, on September 23 in a case of mistaken identity. In his brief, four-year career, Bostock had compiled a .311 batting average.

The personal high achieved in the league that year was Rod Carew's seventh batting title, brought home with a .333 average. This tied Carew with Rogers Hornsby and Stan Musial, while only Honus Wagner with eight and Ty Cobb with twelve batting championships stood ahead of him.

In 1979 Earl Weaver broke the Yankees' three-year grip on eastern honors by hoisting his Baltimore Orioles into first place. Featuring a 20-game winner for the twelfth straight season in lefty Mike Flanagan, who was 23–9, the Orioles banged out 181 home runs, led by Ken Singleton's 35 and 25 apiece from youngsters Gary Roenicke and Eddie Murray, both products of the Orioles' fecund farm system.

A heavy-hitting Milwaukee team finished second, eight games out, hampered by a shortage of top-line pitching. The Brewers had the home run champ in free-swinging Gorman Thomas (45 homers, 175 strikeouts) and received solid hitting from Cecil Cooper (.308), Paul Molitor (.322), and Sixto Lezcano (.321). Ben Oglivie served notice of his arrival with 29 homers and a .282 batting average, while shortstop Robin Yount, at the age of twenty-three already a six-year veteran, was one of the league's outstanding players.

Pitching was also the bête noire of the Red Sox, whose big bats outthumped Milwaukee's. It was a twin-batting show in the outfield through most of the year. Fred Lynn led the league with a .333 average, hit 39 home runs, drove in 122. Jim Rice batted .325, matched Lynn with 39 long ones, and drove in 130 runs.

The Yankees dropped to fourth place despite a 21–9 season from free agent pickup Tommy John and an 18–8 year by Guidry. But the staff was crippled by injuries to Figueroa and Gossage and a 2–9 record by Hunter, at career's end now. The injury to Gossage oc-

curred in the Yankee clubhouse after a game. An innocent exchange of quips with reserve player Cliff Johnson led to a punch-out in which Gossage hurt his thumb. With their incomparable reliever out for several months, the New Yorkers lost their shot at making it four in a row. And to no one's surprise, Cliff Johnson soon packed his bags and went elsewhere, finishing his summer in Cleveland, probably the harshest punishment the team could conjure for him.

California owner Gene Autry's free-spending finally brought a division title to the Angels in 1979. The key man was Rod Carew, signed for megabucks after departing from the Twins. Hampered by a finger injury, Carew "slumped" to .318, but he was part of a solid up-and-down-the-lineup attack that featured Bobby Grich, Carney Lansford, Dan Ford, Willie Aikens, Brian Downing, and Don Baylor. Baylor delivered a mighty season, hitting 36 homers and driving in 139 runs, and running away with the MVP Award.

The Angels, however, couldn't make it all the way to the top, being stopped by the Orioles in four games in the championship series.

The Yankees fought off a tough, stubborn Oriole team to take the title back in 1980. The Orioles got fine offensive seasons again from Singleton and Eddie Murray, now one of the league's best, and showed up with two more 20-game winners in Steve Stone (25–7) and Scott McGregor (20–8).

The Yankees, however, got a 22–9 season from Tommy John, 17–10 from Guidry, 15–5 from ERA titlist Rudy May, and awesome relief work from Gossage and Ron Davis. Reggie Jackson turned in his first .300 season (right on the nose) and sweetened it with 41 homers and 111 runs batted in. Reggie was tied for the four-bagger lead by Milwaukee's Ben Oglivie. The Brewers, still smashing away, banged out 203 home runs, including 38 by Gorman Thomas, 25 by Cecil Cooper, and 23 by Robin Yount.

Cooper turned in a tremendous all-round

hitting performance. Along with his 25 home runs, he batted .352, collected 219 hits, and led the league with 122 runs batted in. But hardly anyone noticed. For this was George Brett's year. Emulating the Rod Carew of 1977, Brett made a spectacular run at .400, ending the season with a .390 mark, baseball's highest batting number since Ted Williams broke the bank with .406 in 1941.

Hampered by nagging foot injuries that limited him to 117 games, Brett swung a mighty bat with metronomic consistency, driving in 118 runs and posting a .664 slugging average, best in the league.

With Brett pounding away and righty Dennis Leonard winning 20 for the third time, the Royals made a shambles of the western division, finishing 14 games up on Oakland, now managed by Billy Martin, a prime example of major-league baseball's hired-fired-hired managerial syndrome. Along with Brett, Kansas City got a spectacular season from outfielder Willie Wilson, a wing-footed switch hitter, who batted .326, stroked 230 hits, and stole 79 bases. But Willie wasn't even close in the legal larceny department. Oakland's twenty-one-year-old speedster Rickey Henderson swiped an even 100 sacks, wiping out Ty Cobb's 1915 American League record of 96.

For the fourth time in five years New York and Kansas City crossed swords in the championship series. This time the Royals came out of the water first, stunning the Yankees in three straight, thanks to strong pitching by Larry Gura, Dennis Leonard, and relief ace Dan Quisenberry. The dramatic moment came in Yankee Stadium in game three. In the top of the seventh, with the Yankees up by 2–1, Gossage came in to face Brett with two men on base. It was 100-mile-an-hour fast balls versus the smoking bat of a .390 hitter. Brett connected with a mighty three-run shot into the Stadium's third deck to seal Kansas City's first pennant.

The American League enjoyed one of the most successful seasons in its history in 1980, drawing nearly 22 million fans, with the National League doing almost as well. The game seemed to be climbing to new heights of national popularity. And then, incredibly, a year later, baseball turned around and gave itself its most stunning black eye since the 1919 World Series scandal by doing the unthinkable—going on strike and stopping the season for nearly two months, from June 12 to August 10. What scandals, a depression, two world wars were unable to do, baseball had done to itself.

The strike had been smoldering for some time, the main issue being compensation for clubs that lost players to free agency, management insisting that the signing team surrender one of its roster players. The players contended that such an arrangement would erode bargaining powers won by them in the free agent market.

The strike was long, costly, and bitter. As the big-league ball parks remained empty week after week, the costs mounted on both sides. Players like the Yankees' recent free agent signee Dave Winfield, whose ten-year contract reportedly called for upward of $20 million (including cost-of-living increases), had an estimated daily loss of around $7,800. Players earning the big-league minimum of $32,500 were losing around $180 per day. The strike was also costly for the clubs. Despite a $50 million strike insurance policy, losses at the turnstiles and concession stands cost the teams well over $100 million. The Yankees, with 25 home dates wiped out, were losing approximately $285,000 per game for an overall estimated loss of slightly over $7 million.

Of equal concern to both players and management was the potential loss in goodwill that the game was suffering. Baseball fans were angry and dismayed at the loss of a diversion that had always filled their summer months with interest, excitement, and recreation.

The positions of both sides hardened and as

time passed it looked as though the remainder of the season might be lost. This fear, along with growing concern about fan disenchantment and indifference (western civilization did not, after all, crumble with the cessation of big-league ball), finally drove both sides to hammer out an agreement at the Doral Inn in New York early on the morning of July 31.

The agreement, a complicated 22-page document, was understood by few. It called for a modest form of compensation for clubs losing free agents, with players being drawn from a pool of talent created by teams wishing to be included in the free agent reentry procedure. At times the agreement sounded like a Chinese menu, with references to Type A players and Type B players.

Naturally, the agreement did not satisfy anyone totally, except for those who, ultimately, really mattered: the fans. When it was announced that after a ten-day mini-spring training period for getting back into shape, the season would resume on August 10, the reaction from fans was generally favorable.

If both labor and management had made a hash of the first part of the 1980 season, the absurdities of the second half were solely the creation of management.

Instead of picking up the season where it had left off, which would have been the logical and sensible thing to do, the lords of baseball came up with one of the most crackbrained schemes imaginable. They decreed it would be a split season, with the first-half division leaders frozen in place and assured a spot in postseason play-offs. If the same team won both halves, it would meet the second-half runner-up in the division play-off. This meant it was possible for the team with the best overall record to not get into the play-offs, which was exactly what happened to the Cincinnati Reds in the National League.

In the American League, the first-half champions were the Yankees in the East, leading by two games over Baltimore, and Oakland in the West, a game and a half better

than Texas. At the end of the second half, Milwaukee had taken the title in the East and Kansas City in the West, setting the stage for a double-tiered set of play-offs: New York versus Milwaukee to determine an eastern division champion and Oakland and Kansas City squaring off to do the same in the West. (As if to emphasize the absurdity of this system, Kansas City had a season's record of 50–53.)

Oakland dropped Kansas City in three straight, while the Yankees defeated Milwaukee in five. New York and Oakland then hooked up to determine the pennant winner. With ex-Yankee skipper Billy Martin managing Oakland, there was an added element of drama to the match. The Yankees, however, with no sense of theater, let the air out of the balloon in the minimum, eliminating the A's in three straight, led by Graig Nettles' nine runs batted in. It was the New York club's thirty-third American League pennant, all of which they had won since 1921, meaning the Yankees had taken 33 flags in 62 years, a success ratio unparalleled by any club in any sport.

With only two thirds of the schedule having been played, some odd-looking statistics went into the record books. Oakland's flash Rickey Henderson led with 135 hits, while Baltimore's Eddie Murray took the RBI title with 78. Almost forgotten by season's end was Oakland's catapult from the gate in April, Martin's club setting a new league record by winning their first 11 games.

For months after the 1981 season was mercifully laid to rest, most of the Hot Stove League speculation centered on the future of Reggie Jackson. Having completed his five-year contract with the Yankees, the game's most conspicuous personality was eligible for free agency once more. While George Steinbrenner remained coyly evasive about his intentions, Reggie and his agent sparred and conferred with several clubs, California and Atlanta most prominently. Finally, on January 22, 1982, much to the dismay of Yankee fans,

Jackson, after waiting for Steinbrenner to make an offer he couldn't refuse, switched teams and coasts, signing a hefty three-year pact with the California Angels.

Letting his big man go was a calculated risk by Steinbrenner. Jackson was not only the Yankees' biggest drawing card and only genuine power threat, but also, undeniably, a winner. Beginning in 1971, Jackson had been on nine division winners in eleven years (five with Oakland, four with New York), with an array of postseason slugging performances that had earned him the appellation "Mr. October." By adding Reggie, the Angels were able to field a lineup that included four past recipients of the American League's Most Valuable Player Award—Fred Lynn, Rod Carew, Don Baylor, and Jackson.

In addition to this luminous array, California's attack included Doug DeCinces, Brian Downing, and Bobby Grich. It was one of baseball's most formidable lineups.

The other muscle-bound batting order in the American League in 1982 belonged to Milwaukee's Brewers in the eastern division. The Brewers' attack was truly fearsome. It included Cecil Cooper, Paul Molitor, Gorman Thomas, Ben Oglivie, Ted Simmons, and Robin Yount. In addition to this power attack, the Milwaukee club had some solid pitchers in right-hander Pete Vukovich, left-hander Mike Caldwell, and Rollie Fingers. Nevertheless, the team got off to a sluggish start and not until Harvey Kuenn replaced Bob Rodgers as manager in early June did they begin winning steadily.

"I just told them to go out there and have fun," the modest Kuenn kept saying all summer as his sluggers did just that, sending shell-shocked pitchers to the showers and earning for themselves the name "Harvey's Wallbangers."

With Jackson gone and with the Yankees employing three managers, five pitching coaches, and three batting instructors during the season, in addition to a constant shuffling of their roster, the Yankees were short-circuited for power, demoralized, confused, and pathetic. Only Dave Winfield had a year to remember (37 home runs, 107 runs batted in).

A tenacious Baltimore club kept nipping at Milwaukee's heels as the division race spooled out in late September. With the Brewers holding a three-game edge over the Orioles, the two teams squared off for a four-game season's finale in Baltimore. Playing spirited ball for their skipper Earl Weaver, whose retirement had been announced before the season, the Orioles stunned the Brewers with three straight wins, sending the two clubs into a tie with one game left to play.

Faced with not just a loss of a division title, but one that would have been painfully humiliating, Milwaukee sent to the mound a recent acquisition from the National League, veteran Don Sutton. Weaver countered with his long-time ace, Jim Palmer. The script dictated a tight game; the Brewers, however, with no sense of drama, came out smoking and thundered away to a 10–2 win.

When the last statistic had been rung up, the Milwaukee hitters stood out as one of the most powerful contingents in recent American League history. Robin Yount batted .331 with 29 home runs, 114 runs batted in, and 210 hits. Cecil Cooper batted .313 with 32 home runs, 121 runs batted in, and 205 hits. Gorman Thomas hit 39 homers and drove in 112 runs. Ben Oglivie hit 32 home runs and drove in 102 runs. Ted Simmons with 97 RBIs just missed being the fifth man to clear the century mark, which would have tied the 1936 Yankees as the only club to have five men driving in over 100 in one season. Paul Molitar batted .302 and collected 201 hits. Overall, the Brewers hit 216 home runs.

In the West, California fought off a tough Kansas City club to take their second division title. Jackson justified his man-sized contract by tying Thomas for the home run lead with 39 and driving in 101 runs. DeCinces hit 30 long ones, batted .301, and drove in 97. Carew swung a .319 bat, while Lynn, Baylor, Downing, Grich, and catcher Bob Boone all turned in strong seasons. Southpaw Geoff Zahn was the big winner for Gene Mauch's club with an 18–8 record.

There were many exciting performances in the league that year, but only one record smasher. This was turned in by Oakland's dynamic base-stealer Rickey Henderson. Henderson not only broke Lou Brock's major-league record of 118 swipes in a single season, but did it with ease and compelling emphasis, and very little suspense (he had, for instance, 84 steals in his first 88 games). By the end of the season he had 130 stolen bases. When Maury Wills stole 104 for the Dodgers in 1962 and set a new record, many people believed that would be the standard for a long time. Twelve years later Brock stole 118. Eight years later, Rickey Henderson bettered Wills by 24 and Brock by 12.

The Brewers made a bit of history of their own in the championship series with California. After dropping the first two games to the Angels in Anaheim, Harvey Kuenn's big bangers came home and became the first team ever in a championship series to sweep three in a row after losing the first two.

After the 1982 season, there were indications that the American League was getting ready to reclaim its primacy. The difference in home run power between the two leagues in 1982 was substantial (even allowing for two extra teams in the American League)—2,080 for the American, 1,299 for the National.

In addition to the established stars like Yount, Thomas, Lynn, Jackson, Carew, Rice, Cooper, Murray, Henderson, Winfield, Willie Wilson, Brett, and others, the American League unveiled in 1982 several outstanding rookies like Baltimore's Cal Ripkin, Boston's Wade Boggs, and Minnesota's Kent Hrbek whose opening seasons were bright with the promise of outstanding careers to come.

The better part of a century has now passed since Ban Johnson defied the odds and the competition and activated his dream by declaring his circuit of teams a major league. Not even the vain and self-confident Johnson could have envisioned the growth and success of the league and the game in which he so passionately believed. In 1901, its first year of operation, the American League's eight pioneers drew just under 1,700,000 paid admissions. In 1982 its fourteen clubs drew over 22,000,000 customers. And this just a year after a strike-interrupted season, when people supposedly became disillusioned with baseball. Disillusioned, perhaps; with baseball, no.

It will go on because of our endless, timeless fascination with what happens to that small white ball with the red stitching.

Don Buford, Baltimore's spark-plug outfielder, who joined the club in 1968 after five years with the White Sox. He retired in 1972 with a .264 career average.

Rollie Fingers early in his career with Oakland, before he grew his famous mustache.

Sal Bando.

Baltimore's four 20-game winners in 1971.

Left to right: Mike Cuellar, Pat Dobson, Dave McNally, Jim Palmer.

Vida Blue.

Gene Tenace.

Joe Coleman, right-handed pitcher and son of Joe Coleman. Young Joe pitched from 1965 to 1979. Pitching for seven different teams, he was a 20-game winner for Detroit in 1971 and 1973. Lifetime he was 142–135.

Bert Campaneris on the prowl.

That blur coming toward Dick Allen's bat is a baseball. From the looks of things, contact was imminent. Allen played from 1963 through 1977, hitting 351 home runs and batting .292.

Bill Melton, White Sox third baseman from 1968 to 1975. Bill led in home runs in 1971 with 33. He batted .253 lifetime.

Aurelio Rodriguez.

Gaylord Perry.

Brooks Robinson.

Rod Carew.

Nolan Ryan.

Jim Palmer.

Luis Tiant.

Carlton Fisk.

Jim Rice.

Bert Blyleven.

Rod Carew on the move.

Fred Lynn.

Andy Messersmith, the man who went to arbitration and opened up the era of free agency. Andy pitched from 1968 to 1979, winning 20 for the Angels in 1971 and 20 for the Dodgers in 1974. Lifetime record: 130–99.

Mark Fidrych.

Lou Piniella.

Wayne Garland.

Bobby Bonds.

Chris Chambliss.

Lyman Bostock.

Dennis Eckersley.

Sparky Lyle.

Thurman Munson. Munson caught for the Yankees from 1969 to 1979, when he lost his life in an airplane crash. He batted .292 lifetime.

Graig Nettles   Reggie Jackson.

Don Baylor.

Bobby Grich.

Boston's Dwight Evans on the way home. The catcher is Cleveland's Gary Alexander. The date, July 9, 1978.

Frank Tanana.

Joe Rudi.

Chicago's Jorge Orta trying to complete a double play and defy the law of gravity at the same time.

Billy Martin.

Dennis Leonard.

Mike Torrez.

Dave Goltz.

Rich ("Goose") Gossage.

Ron Guidry.

Jason Thompson.

Mike Flanagan.

Bucky Dent.

Eddie Murray.

Bob Stanley.

Ken Singleton.

Bobby Murcer.

Tommy John.

Carney Lansford.

Buddy Bell.

Ron LeFlore.

Larry Hisle.

Scott McGregor.

Toby Harrah.

Hal McRae.

Frank White.

Willie Wilson.

George Brett.

Richie Zisk.

Jerry Koosman.

Doug DeCinces.

Jack Morris.

Amos Otis.

Jim Palmer.   Dan Quisenberry.

Steve Kemp.

Jim Sundberg.

Dave Winfield.

Rollie Fingers.

Mike Caldwell.

Cecil Cooper.

Ben Oglivie.

Gorman Thomas.

Robin Yount.

Paul Molitor.

Kent Hrbek.

Rickey Henderson.

Reggie Jackson.

Index